PMP Study Guide

Simplified Exam Prep to Achieve Project Management Professional Certification | Scenario-Based Questions and Detailed Answer Keys

Matthew Maurice

COPYRIGHT PROTECTED
Protected With
ProtectMyWork.com
ALL RIGHTS RESERVED

TABLE OF CONTENTS

INTRODUCTION

As difficult as it may be to think, PMP preparation can be straightforward. The best way to earn your PMP certification and maintain your sanity is not to buy as many study resources as possible and go through endless pages and books.

By simplifying the most complex project management ideas into clear, basic explanations that are easy to remember, this book is intended to cover both the theoretical and practical components of the test. It also gives you enough practice questions to ensure you are properly prepared. The objective is to support you in having a thorough preparation experience free from the typical tension and exhaustion of PMP studying.

Even though the PMP exam can be challenging to pass, you don't need to use the most difficult study materials you can find. The Essential PMP Preparation information is organized logically, making it simple to move from one area to the next and from one subject to the next. You won't have any trouble understanding any of the concepts used, and you'll have the chance to put what you've learned into practice along the way.

The presentation of technically accurate content and making sure it is done in an accessible and lucid manner were the two goals in mind when this book was being developed. By doing this, you can avoid struggling with the typical PMP preparation resources' dense content and difficult academic language.

The PMBOK 7th edition and other sources recommended by PMI in the PMP reference list, such as the Agile Practice Book, are all incorporated in one comprehensive guide, making it the greatest study tool for anyone preparing for the PMP exam.

This study guide is intended to aid you in understanding the terminology used in the People, Process, and Business Environment domains of the PMP exam. Predictive, agile, and hybrid approaches are all covered in-depth in the Essential PMP Preparation. The book offers a comprehensive preparation resource, including practice questions and theoretical information.

Aiming to assist PMP candidates in learning more quickly and retaining information more easily, this self-study book highlights essential terms to help you concentrate and control your pace as you read through each subject. A practice exam of 15 questions designed to gauge your understanding of each project management performance domain follows each chapter. As a last step to assess your exam readiness, you will be given a full-length mock exam at the end of the book in addition to 8 practice exams.

The general introduction to project management and the PMP comes first in this book. A chapter of the book is devoted to exam preparation advice, including best practices, pointers for effective study, advice on time management, and a list of all the Dos and Don'ts that a PMP candidate should pay close attention to before the exam day, on the exam day, and while taking the exam, whether they're taking it in person or online. This chapter also addresses the psychological aspects of the PMP preparation journey by describing how to become and stay motivated and manage stress to ultimately get into the ideal mentality for passing the certification exam.

With the publication of our earlier PMP books, we assisted hundreds of candidates for the certification in achieving their objectives. We achieved this by holding our study resources, including the Essential PMP Preparation, to a high standard.

CHAPTER 1:
Overview

Overview Of Project Management

What Is Project Management?

Can someone genuinely describe how to manage anything before they clearly understand what that thing is? It won't be feasible at all. In our situation, you must first comprehend a project before you can discuss project management.

So What Exactly Is A Project?

Consider it a short-term project with a set beginning and ending time and a predetermined outcome, such as developing a distinctive good or service. In summary, a project is an undertaking with a specified scope, resources allocated particularly for its implementation, and a predictable result. See why it is referred regarded as being transitory?

Additionally, consider a project a singular undertaking because nothing is routine, and the exact operations involved are designed to assist you in achieving a specified goal. When working on a project, you typically assemble a team of individuals with whom you wouldn't typically collaborate and who perform various tasks on other days. They may even be individuals who often reside in various geographic regions and most likely work for several companies.

Examples of Projects

With the explanation given above, you will be able to see how the undertakings below fit the bill, hence qualifying to be termed as projects:

- Construction of a specific bridge
- Construction of a specific building
- Development of some specific software meant to improve business
- Organized relief efforts following some natural disaster
- Introduction of a product into a new geographical market

Some factors that are pertinent to a project include:

- Achieving the intended integration
- Timely delivery of results
- Achieving the learning intended
- Keeping within the budget

The project needs to be managed expertly if the goals mentioned earlier are to be met.

So, Project management: What Is It?

The essence of project management may be summed up as doing whatever is required, including using knowledge, skills, and tools as well as employing the proper protocols to carry out the project's operations in accordance with the essential specifications. As you can see, project management is something that many people perform informally and that you may have done once, twice, or even multiple times without necessarily understanding what it entails.

However, it is best to approach particular initiatives formally, especially when substantial resources are at stake. In any event, resources are constantly limited in today's society, so you want to make sure you are using what you have. In this manner, you can achieve despite having few resources and manage to do a lot. In the middle of the 20th century, project management underwent formalization and was treated seriously.

If we divide project management into semi-independent stages, it will be quite simple to comprehend.

Here Are the Stages of Project Management

The main stages in project management are broadly five. They include:

1. The initiating stage
2. The planning stage
3. The stage of execution
4. The stage of monitoring as well as controlling
5. The closing stage

Now, you might do many things with your resources, even as an organization. If you don't have a methodical technique to weigh your options, you can start initiatives that won't benefit your business the most. The six main reasons are what project management experts suggest you examine.

Here they are:

Demand in the market

You start a project responding to market demand to meet an unmet need. For example, you don't start manufacturing a line of goods and then hunting for customers. An excellent example is when a nation recognizes that its population does not have access to enough power or that it is too expensive for the majority of them. There are solid grounds for starting this alternative power plant. The government may launch a wind-based power project if the nation primarily uses hydroelectric power.

Public organizations or private businesses may decide that investing in water recycling facilities is worthwhile if clean water supplies are becoming exhausted or if their supply cannot keep up with an expanding population. There is a need in both of these situations. The output, in this example, less expensive power and pure water, is ready for the market.

But generally speaking, how can you determine whether there is a need for your proposed good or service? Soon, we'll discuss that.

Business related need

When we talk about a need being business-related, we mean the kind of necessity where other businesses find it vital to use your service or product. Starting a project for the service is worthwhile if employing it increases a business' credibility with clients, increases its efficiency to the point that it allows it to outperform the competition easily, or significantly enhances how it serves businesses.

Consider the ISO accreditation, which is the recognition provided to an organization by the International Organization for Standardization for upholding high-quality standards, for commendable instances in this area. You can start a project to get ISO certification, knowing that doing business of significance will probably make you the go-to company. Here, we're discussing a company's reputation and visibility.

You might also conceive of a Database Management System (DMS) as a project that, if completed, would increase the effectiveness of your company's operations by enabling quick access to accurate data. Remember that when you receive crucial information quickly, you can take advantage of business possibilities before many of your rivals. You would be justified in viewing this part of a business necessity as a strategic opportunity. It means you are starting the project to position yourself for success in the future.

Specific Customer Order

If your company is in the woodworking business, why wouldn't you start making a particular quantity of chairs if a client requested them? Even though you typically create a variety of wooden goods, this time, you will focus precisely on the number of chairs this consumer requests and create them following their preferences

Technology based project

Who among investors wants their companies to carry on conducting business the old-fashioned manual way when every other company is computerized and conducting everyday business electronically? One who is not forward-thinking and ambitious... However, to be effective today—in business, research, or any other endeavor—a person must be able to select the right technology. As a result, both individuals and companies constantly start new technology-related projects.

Legal obligation

Launching certain projects to comply with a legal obligation or necessity is necessary. Shrewd businesspeople identify a commercial opportunity when, for example, the government enacts legislation requiring speed governors to be installed in all public vehicles. They then launch enterprises to produce governors. Such projects wouldn't be necessary if the government didn't make it a requirement that the devices be installed in vehicles used for public transportation. Therefore, it can be said that projects falling under this category are started thanks to the law.

The same situation occurred recently as most nations switched from analog to digital television operations. As a result, business owners worldwide have started initiatives to produce digital boxes for sale to individuals so they can use them in their homes and places of work for TV digitalization.

Social Need

This necessity spurs people to start an endeavor that benefits them or the community. For example, it makes sense for parents to consider starting a project to construct shelters in the sites where their children can congregate while waiting for the school bus or another vehicle that transports them to and from school. Given that it may rain while the kids wait for the bus for a few minutes, this situation has an automatic social need. Additionally, some might want to sit down since they are too exhausted to continue standing, which is why a good shelter is needed.

The Project Management Institute oversees granting project managers the title of "Project Management Professional," which is an accepted professional designation on a global scale. The distinction was created in 1984 and now counts over 900,000 active PMP® award-holders in 218 countries and territories.

The minimum requirements necessary to attain the PMP® designation are as follows:

- **Educational Requirement:** At a minimum, a high school or secondary school diploma is required.
- **Project Management Experience Requirement:**
- If you have an undergraduate university degree or equivalent: 4500 hours spanning 36 months of professional experience (i.e., working in a project management role). Professionalism is key; managing your teammates on a school project does not count.
- If you have only a high school or secondary school diploma: 7500 hours spanning 60 months of professional experience (i.e., working in a project management role).
- **Project Management Education:** 35 hours of formal training in project administration.
- **Ethical Requirement:** By signing it, you agree to the PMI's code of ethics and professional behavior.
- **Exam Requirement:** Taking the PMP® exam is the final requirement; the other minimum requirements must be completed to reach this stage.

Common Reasons For Failed Projects

Why should you get knowledgeable about project execution when you have a solid plan in place? A good plan is good to look at and envisage using, but when it comes to carrying out a project, it is only as good as its implementers. You will be all right if they know how to carry out the plan's specified steps correctly, with room for modifications. Even the best-laid plans can fail if the project manager lacks leadership skills or is egotistical.

You must be aware of the mistakes you should never make as a project manager. In other words, once you are aware of the primary flaws that lead to project failure, you will be aware of them as your project is being carried out, and you will be able to avoid them. The following are the primary causes of project failure, according to numerous studies by the Project Management Institute and schools like Carnegie Mellon University:

Objectives being vague or poorly defined

How would you determine whether you are on the correct road if it is unclear what your project should look like at different stages? When there is a lack of direction, you may not discover the shortcomings of your final product until it is too late to make improvements.

Shaky project sponsorship

Make sure the finances you have budgeted for are accessible as and when you need them if you want your project to be successful. If not, your project can be delayed or possibly fail.

Poor leadership

Even if you don't have many social skills, you must try to maintain open lines of communication if you accept the project manager position. If you are not approachable, your team members won't come to you with their issues until it is sometimes too late, and you will have to solve them for them.

Having a project manager without relevant skills

If the lead sheep in your flock is limping, how far do you think the other sheep can go? Similarly, if the project manager is underqualified and lacks the experience to make up for this, the project will not succeed.

Poorly covered scope

Your team can work hard but outside your project's parameters if you act impulsively throughout project execution rather than sticking to your predetermined plan. Furthermore, anything that is unnecessary to your particular endeavor is useless.

Poor handling of changes

The team's reaction is crucial if adjustments need to be made during the project, whether structural or not. Even though it is necessary to alter the initial strategy somewhat, you still want your team to be united behind the same goal.

Poor definition of project requirements

Who is to ensure that you won't receive supplies of the wrong sizes, the wrong quality, or something else equally problematic if you quote your supplies in general terms, for instance? Exploring your requirements is the only way to ensure all parties follow the strategy. The same logic also holds for demands like timing. If a timeline is specified, your team will work to adhere to it; otherwise, the project will be delayed, and you will suffer unforeseen costs.

Failure to consult with other stakeholders

Project management is not something you can do alone. If you act in such a way just because you are the project manager, you risk being undermined by your team or other interested parties. How will you complete your project if management does not approve certain payments, for instance, if you do not engage upper management over funding?

Failing to put a plan in place to handle risks

Do you anticipate experiencing a catastrophe while working on your project? Then, is it possible to tell? It isn't. You would take all logical precautions to prevent a risk if you were aware of it. However, you can prepare for unforeseen difficulties by setting aside cash for things like resolving unforeseen issues, hiring outside help, etc.

Having an unrealistic budget

It will be like shooting yourself in the foot if you understate your project budget so management can approve its funding. The same people will be present when you ask for more money, and you will probably struggle to convince them that your initial vote wasn't wasted.

These are some of the flaws that cause initiatives to fail now. What can you do particularly to improve your project's chances of success?

Overview Of the PMP Exam

The exam is widely offered in a proctored computer-based testing environment through one of PMI's testing partners (e.g., PearsonVUE, Prometric). For people with specific requirements, paper-based proctored tests and other accommodations are offered. Please contact PMI® or the appropriate testing partner for more details about the exam environment. The exam itself is:

- Closed-book. A physical calculator and paper for notes will be provided for those writing the paper-based exam. Same for the more common computerized exam, except the calculator is a virtual one on the computer.
- 200 multiple-choice questions with a total of 4 answers make up this test. However, 25 of these questions are illustrative questions that are intended to gauge the level of difficulty of potential exam problems. The exam's 25 sample questions are dispersed at random and are not evaluated. As a result, it will be impossible for you to identify which questions are example questions. Therefore, even though you will only be scored on 175 of the 200 questions, treat each of them seriously.
- 4 hours in length inclusive of breaks. As discussed in the exam tips, time management is very important; if you take breaks, this will be on your exam time.
- Graded by "sound psychometric analysis". There is no static passing score for the exam, and it changes from year to year. When you complete the exam, you will only know whether you passed or failed. In your detailed exam report, you will only know how you did in each performance domain relative to the exam population Comprised of 3 prescribed performance domains effective as of July 2020:
- People (42% focus on an exam)
- Process (50% focus on an exam)
- Business Environment (8% focus on an exam)

CHAPTER 2:
About The Exam

The Exam Focus

One of PMI's testing partners offers the exam frequently in a proctored computer-based testing environment (e.g. PearsonVUE, Prometric). Exams can be proctored on paper, and there are also special accommodations for people who need them. The actual test is:

- Closed-book. For those taking the paper-based exam, paper for notes and a physical calculator will be provided. The calculator on the computer is a virtual one for the more widely used computerized exam.
- This exam consists of 200 multiple-choice questions, each of which has four possible answers. However, 25 of these questions are samples that are meant to determine the degree of difficulty of potential questions that could be used in future exams. The 25 practice questions are sprinkled throughout the exam at random, but they are not evaluated. As a result, you won't be able to determine which questions are example questions. Even though only 175 of the 200 questions will have an impact on your final score, you should still answer each one carefully.
- 4 hours total, including breaks. Time management is crucial for exams, and if you do take breaks, this will take away from your exam time, as will be covered in the exam recommendations.
- "Sound psychometric analysis" was used to grade. The exam has a dynamic passing score that varies from year to year. When you finish the exam, you will only know if you passed or failed, and your thorough exam report will only explain how you performed relative to the exam population in each performance domain (i.e. comparably above average, average, or below average).
- Comprised of 3 prescribed performance domains effective as of July 2020:

- People (42% focus on the exam)
- Process (50% focus on the exam)
- Business Environment (8% focus of exam)

The New PMP Exam Course Content

Although it probably doesn't apply to you, there is a paper-based version of the PMP exam that is available. However, it's only available to applicants who live at least 240 kilometers or more away from the nearest Prometric testing center or live in a country that doesn't have a testing center at all, and where crossing the border would be either prohibited or unduly burdensome, at the discretion of PMI. In the case of paper-based tests, you do not receive a notification immediately of whether you've passed or failed. Rather results are sent by email six to eight weeks after finishing up the test.

This is the most likely scenario as there are thousands of test centers available in over 180 countries around the world. Furthermore, an additional benefit of center-based testing is that you'll receive a printed copy of your test results immediately after completing your exam so that you can begin calling yourself a PMP that very day, given that you've completed it.

While the PMP exam is given in English by default, there are accommodations available for those who might be more comfortable in a different language. If requested at the time of application, translations are available at no additional cost and appear below each question and answer on the exam. Arabic, Brazilian Portuguese, Chinese (both simplified and traditional), French, German, Hebrew, Italian, Japanese, Korean, Polish, Russian, Spanish, and Turkish are among the options you have. Accommodations may be made for a range of disabilities, handicaps, and other impairments in addition to linguistic needs. You need to request these accommodations before scheduling your exam and you should prepare medical documentation for PMI to review. There's no additional cost to these accommodations, so long as you and PMI can come to an arrangement that allows you to have the greatest chance of success in taking the exam. When it comes time to pay the exam fee, the standard rate is either $555 or 465 euros.

However, there is a discounted rate available for members of the Project Management Institute, at either $405 or 340 euros. When it comes to renewal, these are only available in dollar denominations, and cost either $150, for the standard rate, or a discounted rate of

$60 if you are a member of PMI. You may pay these exam fees using either a credit card, online, or by mail, as well as a money order, check, or wire transfer. Now, I mentioned that there is a discounted rate available if you are a member of PMI, and I strongly encourage joining PMI, at least for your first year while you're preparing for the PMP exam. Membership dues are $129 per year, in addition to a $10 application fee. Student member dues are also available for those who might be in a full-time degree-granting accredited college or university program, for only $32 a year, making that a great bargain if you happen to fall into that category.

Additionally, there are chapter dues available for your local chapter with dues ranging from zero to $60 per year, and most chapters charge $25 to $35 to help fund local events and local speakers, pay for meeting spaces for members to get together, and so on. Among the key benefits of joining PMI is a digital copy of the PMBOK Guide, which is at minimum $65 or so valuable, and an essential tool as you study for the PMP exam. Further, you'll gain access to digital copies of all of PMI's global standards, as well as access to a library of study guides and practice tests, and access to project management books, tools, and templates. In addition to subscriptions to several different PMI publications. If you go in and do the math, and simply add the member exam fee rate to the PMI membership rate for a year, you arrive at a total of $534, which is less than the standard exam fee would be on its own. Plus, you're already in a lot better financial position than you would be if you didn't join PMI just by receiving that free copy of the PMBOK Guide. Of course, there is a purpose for how everything is set up.

PMI wants you to sign up and, ideally, get involved with their local chapter. Increasing your chances for networking and for learning more about project management.

Exam Prerequisites

The exact prerequisites you need to fill in before taking the PMP Exam to vary a bit depending on your educational background. Having a secondary degree, high school certificate, associate degree, or its equivalent on a global scale, or having completed a four-year degree or a higher level of education, is what distinguishes you from other candidates. This could be your master's or Doctoral-level coursework, as well as your Bachelor's degree and its equivalent internationally. We would discover that the prerequisites for taking the exam, based on having a secondary degree, include 7500 hours of project management experience, dispersed over at least a time of 60 total months. Additionally, you'll need 35 hours of formal training before sitting for the exam. These requirements vary a bit if you have a Four-Year Degree with a lower 4500 hours required of Project Management experience, instead of 7500, as well as only 36 months of Project Management experience, rather than the 60 that might be required if you only had a Secondary Degree.

However, that requirement of 35 hours of Formal Project Management Training remains the same, and applies equally, regardless of your education level. Any of the various project management knowledge areas, such as project integration, scope, schedule, cost, quality, resource, communications, risk, procurement, or stakeholder management, may be covered in this training. You can obtain these 35 hours of training from several different places as well. Any local PMI chapters and communities of practice, any employer- or company-sponsored programs, training firms, or, experts, as well as any PMI Registered Education Providers or R.E.Ps.

Distance-learning companies that include an end-of-course assessment as part of their curriculum, as well as any university or college academic and continuing education programs regarding Project Management material. You may additionally include any fraction of a course that you might take, for example at a university that covers Project Management even if that's not the focus of the overall class. For example, if you were in an accounting course that meets for three hours each week for ten weeks, and you spend six of those hours on Project Management related accounting practices, then you could count those six hours as part of your training. However, it's always best to get your training from a source that can provide a holistic look at what is going to be found on the exam and can help best prepare you for success. So, if you already have the experience requirements in place, and the sufficient education level and background, then all you need to fulfill the training requirement for the exam is to work your way through this learning path.

Question Patterns

So now that you better understand the requirements to take the PMP Exam, what can you expect from the test itself? The PMP Exam is composed of 200 questions overall. 25 of which go unscored, leaving 175 to be scored. Test versions in the future may include experimental queries. Unscored questions are present in this test, as they are in many other standardized exams, but the test-taker has no way of knowing for sure whether a particular question will be scored or not.

Therefore, it's crucial to answer all 200 inquiries truthfully and completely. The overall time allotted for you to complete all 200 of these questions is four hours. There are no planned breaks, but you can stop if you need to use the bathroom or get a drink of water.

At least for the vast bulk of those who take it, it is a computer-based test. For those who might be too far from testing locations, there is a paper-based version that we'll cover in the following module. However, because Prometric has thousands of testing locations worldwide, it is extremely unlikely that you would need to take the paper-based version of the exam. The test is not adaptive in nature, so it does not become tougher or easier as the test progresses based on how you are answering the questions. Additionally, as I already stated, there is no way to predict which questions will be scored or not because they are distributed randomly throughout the exam.

To establish what might constitute a passing score for the test, PMI claims that the test is watched through what they refer to as psychometric analysis. In essence, in my opinion, this means that questions are ranked according to overall difficulty and that your exam is probably put together from a broader pool of potential test questions. The passing threshold may be adjusted slightly by how difficult or easy the questions on your exam are.

In any event, international work groups of PMP credential holders create and independently validate the PMP Exam. This test and credential were created by project managers for project managers, as I already stated. And that holds for the test just as much as it does for anything else. The five distinct process groups that we discussed in the prior module make up the exam content. Initiation-related questions make up 13% of the exam questions, and project-planning questions make up 24%. 25 percent of the project life cycle is devoted to monitoring and controlling procedures that we may use, while 31% is concerned with carrying out project responsibilities.

Finally, the remaining seven percent of the questions are dedicated to closing tasks that occur either at the end of the project phases or at the end of our project's work in its entirety. While this breakdown of questions is unequal in nature, it does roughly follow the amount of effort and work that's been in any particular phase of our project's work. After all, after spending some time in initiation, and more time in planning out our project, the vast majority of our activities are going to take place in completing the project work itself. Similarly, we're going to have to spend a lot of time conducting monitoring and controlling throughout the entirety of the project life cycle. As such, planning, executing, monitoring, and controlling are worth the extra attention that they receive given that that's where the majority of your time as a Project Manager will be spent as well.

Let's take a moment to review. The experience requirement that must be met before applying for the PMP Exam varies based on your educational background. If you only have a high school diploma or an Associate's Degree, or its global equivalent, then you're going to have to have a higher level of overall project management experience than is required if you come into the exam application with either a four-year degree or higher. Something like a Bachelor's, Master's, or Doctorate. Regardless of this educational background requirement, the training requirement is the same for all exam applicants. It's required that you undertake at least 35 hours of training specifically related to project management subjects. It is also possible to use training from PMI chapters, employer programs, other and training organizations, as well as pertinent college courses, provided that the course content is pertinent to the PMP Exam. Regarding that, there are 200 total topics on the PMP Exam. 25 unscored items are sprinkled throughout the test, out of the 175 that are scored.

The exam takes place over a period of up to four hours, and is computer-based in nature, as well as multiple choice. However, it's not adaptive, meaning it doesn't get harder or easier while you go through the exam the way an exam like the GMAT might. The vast majority of questions focus on planning, executing, monitoring, and controlling processes, given that's where the majority of your time will also be spent as a Project Manager. We'll examine the PMP exam process in greater detail in the following module. If you've satisfied the criteria covered in this session, you'll need to know how to apply for the exam and reserve a test date. I'll be glad to see you then.

Study Tips

The general study advice listed below should be kept in mind while you get ready for the test. Please keep in mind that every person is unique, so if you have a strategy that works best for you, stay with it.

- **Understand the Big Picture.** You won't be able to memorize everything in the book unless you have an exceptionally strong memory. Additionally, the exam assesses understanding of the content through application in addition to knowledge of the material (i.e., scenario-based questions). You want to work wisely and study effectively keeping this in mind as well as any other restrictions you may have, such as a short prep period.

For instance, 49 processes are dispersed across 10 knowledge domains and 5 process categories. Think about how each position enhances the others. Think about questioning yourself: Which steps must be completed first? Which methods are parallel processing supported? If you have a mental framework to guide you in extracting the crucial information and using it during the test, it will be simpler for you to apply your knowledge.

- **Look for the Why Factor.** Continue with the prior advice by making an effort to comprehend the rationale behind each idea. How will this help me with my project, for example? What benefit does this offer? When trying to weed out answers on the exam, understanding why something is done can be helpful.
- **Memorize Formulae.** Since the exam is a closed book, if anything is to be memorized it is all the formulae. Use the formula sheet after the exam tip section to help you memorize.
- **Familiarize yourself with the Lingo.** Numerous terms are either specific to project management or have their definitions in that context. You can more effectively decode a question to comprehend what it is asking if you are aware of the language and how it is used.
- **View Concrete Examples.** To speed up and reinforce your learning, look at instances in addition to the spoken definitions and explanations of concepts. The proverb "A picture is worth a thousand words" comes to mind.
- **Complete lots of Practice Questions.** The best way to master any skill is with practice and repetition. However, if you don't understand the question, don't waste your time and review the material first.
- **Target Weaknesses.** Practice questions can help identify your weak points (i.e. questions you got wrong or had to guess). Make the most of things and develop those areas into strengths.

Exam Tips

The following are exam tips and strategies to consider when completing the exam. This section is divided into pre-exam tips, exam tips, and exam strategies.

Pre-Exam Tips:

- **Prepare Logistically.** Make sure you choose an exam date that provides you with adequate preparation time. Try visiting your test center in advance to familiarize yourself with the location and environment.

- **Have a Good Night's Sleep.** Studies have shown that trying to pull an all-nighter to cram before an exam can do more harm than good, especially, when many of the questions involve critical thinking as opposed to pure memory recall.
- **Have a Wholesome Breakfast.** Making ensuring you have enough energy to get through the exam is important. Moreover, you should try to avoid getting hungry while taking the exam as this could distract you and make you waste time getting a snack.
- **Don't Forget Anything.** Make sure you have the necessary photo ID and exam confirmation required for check-in. Also, bring water and light snacks in case you do need a short break (these items would be stored in a mini locker or alternative area at the test center).
- **Arrive Early.** Make careful to arrive between 30 and 45 minutes before the exam begins. Check-in and processing times may be prolonged at test centers because several separate exams are frequently scheduled for the same time. Additionally, you should account for that wiggle room in case of uncertain unknowns.
- **Be Confident.** If you go into the exam uncertain and fearful of failure then you may fall into a self-fulfilled prophecy trap. If you take the opposite approach and go in optimistic about your success, you increase your inner stability and focus which will help you through the exam.

Exam Tips:

- **Manage your Time.** Time management is one of the most effective tips in project management and the same applies to the exam. Two key ways this can be done:
- **Stay on Pace and Keep Moving.** Avoid spending too much time on one thing. Keep in mind that each inquiry will last, on average, 72 seconds. Make your best estimate and flag the question for later review, if time allows, if you find a question is taking up too much time.
- **Use Spare Time to Review Flagged Questions.** Save the hard questions that you have flagged for further review if you have time. If you don't have enough

time, it's not the end of the world, since you already guessed if you followed the preceding advice.

- **Minimize Breaks.** Only take a break if you need to (e.g. washroom breaks, stretching breaks for improved circulation, sanity breaks for peace of mind). Try to avoid drinking too much water before the exam to avoid frequent washroom breaks.
- **Read Carefully.** Some of the exam questions can be quite wordy, so try to avoid skimming through and answering prematurely. Two pro tips:
- **Beware of Shifts.** A common trap in wordy questions, watch out for questions that shift perspective or focus part-way through or right at the end. These questions will provide context and have you thinking about Concept A. Then the shift will occur and the question will ask about Concept B. However, if you don't read the full question, you'll miss it and answer incorrectly.
- **Leverage Context and Language.** Whenever you're stumped and don't know the meaning of a word, try to use the context of the question and prefixes or suffixes to help get the gist of the meaning.
- **Consider the Queries to be true.** Don't overinterpret the questions. Avoid attempting to read between the lines and unduly taking into account other factors because the questions will be straightforward and plain.
- **Benchmark to Previous Questions.** In some cases, you may find one question provides further insight into another completely unrelated question by coincidence. For example, one question may be centered on the best technique to be used in a situation and another question will define one of the candidate techniques.
- **Answer all Questions.** Leave no question unanswered, even if you have to blindly guess in a desperate last-minute time crunch (hopefully, your time management is commendable enough to avoid this scenario).
- **Manage Emotions.** Try to avoid exam anxiety with rehearsed breathing exercises and keeping a positive frame of mind. Sometimes the sheer scale and the number of questions can be overwhelming. In this scenario, just focus on one question at a time and chip away the best you can. Know yourself and what coping strategies work best to keep you calm during exams.

Exam Strategies:

- **Easy Questions First.** Set a hard time constraint per question to help you stay on track (e.g., 60 seconds). An easy question is where you can confidently make your best selection within this period. If you can't answer within this period then make the best guess and flag the question. If you adhere to this time-boxing strategy then you should have some time left at the end to mull over the tougher questions. Some studies do indicate that the first best guess is usually more correct than later changes to the first best guess. So, beware of doubting yourself and only change the first best guess if you have a really good reason to do so.
- **The elimination process.** Your odds of making the correct prediction with this method can significantly rise. If you make a wild guess, you have a 1/4, or 25%, chance of being correct. But, you will have a 50% probability of correctly guessing the answer if you can rule out two possibilities, which is a considerably better chance than a 25% chance.
- **Avoid Fact Traps.** Avoid giving true but unrelated answers to the topic at hand. A response does not necessarily answer the question just because it is accurate in general. These kinds of responses function as distractions.
- **Avoid Extremities.** Answers that use words like "never" and "always" to express absolute views are more likely to be untrue. The simplest method to evaluate the accuracy of one of these responses is to come up with a counterexample.
- **Leverage Answer Choice Families.** Some questions may have two or more answers that are similar in nature and construction. Two of those answers may also be direct opposites of each other. For example, one answer may state "the CPI increases" while another answer may state "the CPI decreases". Usually in these cases, one of the answers in this family will be the correct answer.

Consistent Blind Guessing. If you are in a mad last-minute rush where there isn't enough time to eliminate answers, instead of guessing at random, choose the same answer consistently (e.g. letter "A"). Each independent question has a ¼ or 25% chance of choosing the right answer when blindly guessing. Nevertheless, if you take a look at a group of questions (like the past ten questions) and believe that the answers are distributed fairly evenly, you may anticipate that if you constantly choose the same letter, you will at least answer 2 to 3 of the questions correctly.

CHAPTER 3:
General PMP

Educational Section Regarding the Topic General PMP

In this chapter, we will discuss the topic of the general PMP educational section and some recommended courses to take to prepare for the exam.

Some of the key examinable topics in General PMP include:

- Planning and controlling a project.
- Identifying project constraints.
- Selecting project resources, including direct cost and indirect cost.
- Developing the stakeholder management plan.
- Marketing the PPM system.
- Analyzing product data to identify trends and changes in various measures such as defect density, lead time, part count, usage, churn rates, etc.
- Measuring project performance.
- Monitoring risk using the periodic risk register and performing periodic risk reassessments to identify emerging and existing risks. Reviewing the risks in the context of the project life cycle and identifying controls for each risk.
- Managing communications channels with stakeholders, team members, and customers by coordinating meetings, presentations, and announcements by scheduling, answering emails, etc.
- Documenting project activities in a structured manner by communicating activities, actions, and change requests for routine tasks e.g.

Constraints

Constraints include anything that can limit the success or potential of your project but still has to be managed to deliver the project successfully.

What is an illustration of a constraint?

Examples: Time, cost, scope, and requirements are the most obvious constraints in project management.

Other examples of constraints include risks, resources, and quality. For example, you may have specific quality metrics that have to be met on your project. Technology can also be a constraint; maybe you must integrate with your company's legacy system or code software in a certain programming language. These are two real examples from my background in IT but think about examples from your own experience that will help you recall the information on the exam.

While preparing for the exam, consider the context of constraints broadly and widely, and consider how they might test you on constraints with a scenario question.

Stakeholders

A simple question such as, "what is a stakeholder?" shouldn't pose any issues for you during the test. However, given different scenarios, your area of focus should be comprehending stakeholders and their level of influence on your project.

A stakeholder, by definition, is anyone with a vested interest in your project that can be either positively or negatively affected. Your project sponsor, community, and project team are examples of stakeholders, including functional managers, operations managers, vendors, customers, PMO, portfolio managers, community, etc.

Progressive Elaboration

The iterative concept of progressive elaboration means the more information and detail you have, the better you can plan the project. For example, in the earliest stages of your project plan, you will not likely have defined requirements, tasks, resources, or accurate estimates. However, as you get further along in your planning process, you have more information and greater accuracy with which you can plan your project.

Rolling Wave Planning

Rolling wave planning involves the iterative nature of planning project work in greater detail in the earlier stages and then planning work at a higher level of detail in later stages. The example of bridge construction can be used to illustrate progressive elaboration. If you are building a bridge, you may be able to define the work for the first six months clearly. You might have less information in months 7 through 18. However, as you approach months 19 through 24, you might only have a cursory grasp of the work involved, making it impossible for you to plan in any level of detail.

Projects, Programs, and Portfolios

You are expected to understand the difference between a project, a portfolio, and a program. You already know that a project is a special, transient undertaking to produce a good, service, or outcome.

But a program is a collection of related tasks that are organized and managed. The initiatives are connected by a central benefit. For instance, during my early corporate career, I managed an end-to-end e-commerce solution team for a large consumer goods firm. For that business, several of the technology projects in question covered various brands. However, I concentrated on overseeing related tasks, maximizing available resources, and coordinating schedules among them. The planning process's objective was to make the entire program better.

A portfolio involves strategic alignment with the company's initiatives, and portfolios may include a blend of programs and projects. If I worked at the portfolio level for that same consumer goods company and were charged with meeting a certain ROI or market share, this would demonstrate an example of strategic alignment with the company's organizational objectives.

For the exam, it is important to understand what it means to manage at the project, program, and portfolio levels. So, think of examples. You don't have to use my examples; find examples that work for you.

Project Governance

Project decisions, such as those that match project outcomes with corporate strategy, are made within the context of project governance. Project governance factors into the project life cycle, phase review, escalation, stakeholder communication, and issue resolution.

Project Management Office

The PMO is a structure that centralizes project management within an organization. The PMO is a project stakeholder focusing on the standardized coordination of project resources, processes, and governance. The primary function of the PMO is to support the project manager. Be aware of exam questions that position the PMO as having a primary function to support a particular stakeholder or organization. Each of these would be incorrect because the PMO supports the project manager.

As you would expect, the structure of the PMO could vary based on the organizational structure. Therefore, the PMO's level of involvement and support given to the project will vary. Also, you must know the different types of PMOs:

- Supportive PMOs have a more consultative approach
- Controlling PMOs focus more on compliance
- Directive PMOs can get heavily involved in managing project

Project and Operations Management

Beyond testing you on the differences between the definitions of projects and operations, PMI expects you to understand when projects intersect with operations. For example, there may be specific operational responsibilities that must be completed at various stages, such as; the project close-out phase, process improvements, operational changes, or product upgrades.

Operations involve ongoing work. You already know the definition of a project, but you need to discern when an exam question is testing you about projects versus operations.

If you are asked to build a fleet of new sports cars, is that a project or operation? Because it is a one-of-a-kind, transient undertaking, the solution is projected. Making new sports cars is an illustration of operations because it is a continuous process. You would anticipate that more than one car would be manufactured because manufacturing is a continuous activity. Based on the example, you can begin to see how PMI might test you on the concept of projects versus operations.

All phases of a project should take operations into account and be included. This may occur when resources are transferred from operations into the project at the project's beginning and when resources and deliverables (verifiable results) are transferred back into operations at the project's conclusion.

Business Value

Business value is referred to as the whole worth of the company, which includes both tangible and intangible assets. Intangibles include things like the brand and intellectual property of your business. Building value is the organizational goal, thus when projects are handed to you, it's because the investments and actions have some value to the organization. Operations help businesses create value.

What Are the Benefits of Becoming a Project Management Professional (PMP)?

Becoming a Certified Project Management Professional will provide you with the following benefits:

Enhances Professional Marketability

Many organizations are now aware of the importance of project management and its role in achieving business objectives. They also see that randomly calling someone a project manager within the organization who manages a project is not enough. Just like information technology, engineering, and other professions, project management has particular skills and qualifications.

Becoming certified will improve your marketability as an important business asset because it tells a potential employer that you have the knowledge, skills, and experience to manage important projects, and of course help, the company achieves its goals.

Earning a prestigious certificate can help you be highly competitive in the job marketplace. If you are a certified project manager and you are competing against a candidate who doesn't hold any certification, there's a high chance that you will be hired.

Hiring managers would often choose candidates who are duly certified over applicants who don't have any certification at all. Certification will demonstrate to your possible employers that you have performed the required work and you have the skills needed to become a highly effective project manager. Also, it demonstrates your commitment to your professional development and respect for standards.

Raises Client Confidence

Like the fact that becoming certified will assure potential employers that you have the background and experience to manage projects, it also brings confidence to your clients that you are a competent and experienced project manager.

Earning your certificate will help your employer sell customers on your capacity to manage important projects. Clients, similar to possible employers, are usually looking for assurance that those they deal with are professional and have the knowledge and skills to perform the duties involved. Project managers who are duly certified will translate their professionalism and ethics into their work. This improves the trust clients will have in you that, in turn, will provide you with the capacity to influence them on pressing project concerns.

Shows Professional Achievement

Becoming a certified project management professional is not easy. It involves an intensive process, which requires documentation of your achievements in managing projects. The certification exam will assess how well you comprehend the project management fundamentals described in the Project Management Body of Knowledge (PMBOK).

Not everyone can take the exam as you need several years of project management experience before you can even sit to take the test. You require 35 hours of formal project management training in addition to professional experience.

Getting a certificate will assure your employers and clients that you have an advanced understanding of project management principles and processes. This demonstrates that you have experience and mastery of project management as a professional discipline.

Offers Opportunities for Professional Growth

Earning your PMP certification shows that you value professional growth, and demonstrates that you are not afraid to go the extra mile to achieve what you want.

For potential employers, a certificate is an indicator that you are a can-do professional who is driven by success. They will have the assumption that you are likely to show the same characteristics on the job, which is important for employers.

Certified PMPs are often seen as success-driven, high-energy professionals, which are usually offered highly rewarding opportunities.

General PMP Questions

1. All but one of the statements made regarding the project plan are accurate:

The project charter:

A) officially confirms a project's existence

B) issued by the project manager or project sponsor/initiator

C) gives the project manager the power to use corporate resources for the project.

D) gives senior management a means of approving and committing to the initiative

2. The Project Charter includes all of the following except:

A) Project purpose or justification

B) High-level requirements

C) Summary budget

D) Project exclusions

3. Sally recently took over Sally's job from a different project manager. Planning for the endeavor is currently underway. Sally is interested in knowing about high-level risks, but the team has not yet begun adding risks to the risk registry. Which supplier is ideal for Sally?

A) Organizational Process Assets

B) Project Assumptions

C) Project Charter

D) Business Case

4. Sara, a Senior project manager for a cable manufacturing company, helped the sponsor create the project charter. She ensured that the project charter was complete and approved and that all stakeholders were familiar with its contents. Who is in charge of approving the project charter?

A) Project Sponsor/initiator/customer

B) Project Manager

C) Functional Manager

D) Project Stakeholders

5. Which subordinate plans from the list below are included in the project management plan? There are numerous choices available.

A) Configuration Management Plan

B) Requirement Management Plan

C) Change Management Plan

D) Process Improvement Plan

6. Fanny is in the planning phase of her project and is preparing the project management plan. Which of the following must Fanny consider incorporating into her plan? There are numerous choices available.

A) Select a life cycle for the project

B) Assumptions and constraints

C) Tailor details of processes to be followed in the project

D) Configuration Management Plan

7. Angela is a new project manager at SeeRight Systems. At which point during the project is it appropriate time for her to use the project management plan? Select all the valid options.

A) While working on creating the deliverables of the project

B) During all planning for creating all subsidiary and controlling processes

C) While monitoring and controlling the work of the project

D) While reviewing/approving or rejecting changes for the project

8. Kate is a project manager in charge of setting up a very large steel plant. Her project is in the planning stage of scope management. Which terms describe the elements that make up the scope baseline?

A) Project Scope Statement

B) WBS

C) WBS Dictionary

D) All of the above

9. Tina is a Senior project manager at Wellfleet Ltd. When she was giving an overview of the company's project

management processes to a group of newly joined project managers, One asked about how and when change requests that get approved by the change control board (CCB) are implemented. Change requests are implemented as part of:

A) Perform Quality Control

B) Monitor and Control Project Work

C) Direct and Manage Project Work

D) Implement integrated change management

10. Daisy is a new project manager at Excavate Mines Ltd. Her project is in the execution phase. Through the project management plan, she has ensured that the project is carried out and progressing. The enterprise also needs to implement a lot of change requests. If she has the Project Management Plan and the required Enterprise Environmental Factors and Organizational Process Assets, what else would she need to ensure 100% completion of work at a particular point in time?

A) Rejected Change Requests

B) Approved Change Requests

C) Change Requests

D) Integration Management Plan

11. As part of the project execution phase, Robert is putting the authorized change requests into practice. What is acceptable as a description of the change requests that have been approved:

A) Corrective Action

B) Preventive Action

C) Defect Repair

D) All of the above

12. Christopher works for a pharmaceutical company. He's a project manager in charge of producing a lifesaving drug at a lower cost than the competition. The success of this project and product is crucial for his organization since it is to increase the company's revenue by a whopping 25%. Due to the complexity of the project, his day is packed with many meetings with various stakeholders. Christopher is using the following best practices to run his meetings, select the invalid one:

A) Meetings are for discussing only relevant topics while directing and managing project work

B) All stakeholders, including the project team, will need to be invited to all meetings

C) Meeting minutes should be stored as defined in the Project Management Plan

D) Virtual meetings require additional preparation to achieve nearly the same experience as a face-to-face meeting

13. As a project manager you know that meetings are very crucial to the day-to-day management of a project. You are also aware that meetings need to be well planned, scheduled, and target the right audience, and that the agenda and minutes need to be circulated after the meeting. Which one of the following project management meeting types has been scientifically proven? Choose all that apply.

A) Information Exchange

B) Brainstorming

C) Decision-making

D) All of the above

14. Rob, a project manager with an automobile design and consulting firm, always takes steps to ensure that all project work is completed. Apart from project deliverables, which product would he produce from the list below as a part of the project execution phase?

A) Work Performance Report

B) Work Performance Data

C) Work Performance Information

D) A and B

15. Henry oversees a data migration project that is currently in the implementation stage. As this is his first experience with data transfer, he is trying to find out more about previous projects that his company has undertaken that are similar to this one. He discovered that the majority of data migration projects had budget overruns and were delayed. Henry was able to gather this information from:

A) Knowledge Database

B) Lessons Learned Database

C) SharePoint

D) Official Intranet

16. Beth is a senior project manager working on a critical mission satellite project for a government agency. She just completed the execution phase of the project and claimed that her execution was 100% complete. She could make this claim based on which of the following:

A) Completion of Deliverables as listed in the Project Charter

B) Completion of detailed Deliverables as listed in the Project Scope Statement

C) Acceptance of project deliverables by the client

D) Completion of project work as detailed in the Project Plan

17. Sarah is the program manager for a data migration project that needs to be completed in 16 months. A change request was raised that would result in a change to the scope baseline, Cost baseline, and schedule baseline of the project. These change requests will get approved as part of which process?

A) Monitoring and Controlling

B) Direct and Manage Project Work

C) Perform Integrated Change Control

D) Control Scope, Control Cost, and Cost Schedule

18. The process of identifying, documenting, and approving or rejecting changes to the project documents, deliverables, and baselines comes under:

A) Configuration Control

B) Change Control Board (CCB)

C) Perform Integrated Change Control

D) Change Control

19. Martha is in charge of a Data Center transformation project and is carrying out the monitoring and controlling processes. It is important for her to verify that the composition of every configuration item in the project is accurate and that any necessary modifications are recorded, assessed, authorized, monitored, and executed. What does she need to report the status to her management?

A) Configuration Audit Results

B) Change Request raised for the changes to be implemented

C) Approval from her senior manager

D) Configuration Status Accounting

20. You oversee a housing development that is constructing houses in an upscale neighborhood. You are now coordinating and supervising the project's work. You need to ensure all the following inputs are available for monitoring and controlling project work except for which of the following:

A) Verified Deliverables

B) Validated Changes

C) Cost Forecasts

D) Schedule Forecasts

General PMP Detailed Answer Keys

1. **ANSWER:** B

The project charter is not issued by the project manager. It is issued only by the project initiator/customer/sponsor. The project manager facilitates the creation of a charter and ensures that all stakeholders are aware of its contents.

2. **ANSWER:** D

Project exclusions, or what the project scope does not include, are stated in the project scope statement after a more detailed analysis.

3. **ANSWER:** C

The high-level risks, if they exist, would be found in the project charter. These can then be recorded in the planning phase of the risk register once it is created.

4. **ANSWER:** A

The project sponsor is responsible for funding the project and approving (signing) the charter. The project manager can facilitate the creation of the charter and is responsible for ensuring that all stakeholders understand the objectives mentioned in the charter.

5. **ANSWER:** All

All options provided are integrated into the project management plan.

6. **ANSWER:** A, C, and D

The project management strategy will not include any of the alternatives besides B. The project charter, project scope statement, and requirements document include assumptions and limitations.

7. **ANSWER:** All

It is appropriate to use the project management plan in all stages listed.

8. **ANSWER:** D

The scope baseline is the version of the scope statement, WBS, and WBS dictionary that has been authorized.

9. **ANSWER:** C

Implementing approved change requests is a part of the "direct and manage project activity" phase of the Executing Process Group.

10. ANSWER: B

The only choices that can be used to direct and manage the project work process are approved change requests. Change requests are another possible output from this procedure.

11. ANSWER: D

Approved changes can be implemented in the form of any of the options provided.

12. ANSWER: B

This is because not all stakeholders need to be present or should be invited to all meetings. Only relevant stakeholders who are involved in the project and affected by the meeting subject need to be present. The project manager, therefore, needs to ensure that all the right people are invited to the right meetings, while at the same time avoiding inviting people who are unaffected by the topic.

13. ANSWER: D

Meetings can be any of the types listed from A-C.

14. ANSWER: B

This is an output of the "direct and manage project work" phase.

15. ANSWER: B

Project files from previous projects would contain documented lessons learned and information regarding the project.

16. ANSWER: C

Deliverables are products, results, or services that are required to complete a phase and or process of the project. Once the client accepts the deliverables, the work is complete. Option C is therefore the only correct answer.

17. ANSWER: C

As part of the integrated change control process, the change control board will review and accept or reject each change request. This is a monitoring and control activity. Option C is therefore the only correct answer.

18. ANSWER: D

The definition of change control is given in the query. Only the change request is subject to CCB's study, evaluation, approval, deferral, or rejection.

Ref: PMBOK5 4.5 Implement integrated change management.

19. ANSWER: A

The question explains the definition of configuration cudit as provided in PMBOK5. Configuration status accounting accounts for when the data related to configuration items should be provided, making option D incorrect. B-C are also invalid options.

Ref: PMBOK5 4.5.1 Perform Integrated Change Control.

20. ANSWER: A

Option A is the correct answer as it is a valid INPUT for the "validate scope" process. This is the process where the client validates deliverables verified by the quality control process. Validated changes are not a valid option as they refer to reviewing approved change requests to ensure they were implemented properly. Schedule forecasts and cost forecasts are not valid options because they are inputs for the monitoring and control process.

CHAPTER 4: Project Integration

Educational Section Regarding the Topic Project Integration

Project Integration management is a collection of processes required to consolidate the processes within the process groups and ensure they are properly coordinated. The accountability of the integration lies with the project manager, and some of the key activities performed by him while performing this are:

- Creating the project charter that justifies the business case for the project and authorizes it. It also gives the project manager authority to work on the project.
- Consolidating the subsidiary plan includes management plans for Scope, Schedule, Cost, Quality, Communication, Risk, Human Resource, Procurement, and Stakeholder Management.
- Acquiring, developing, and managing the team to achieve what is required
- Conducting procurement if required in the project
- Closing the project/phase

According to PMBOK, Project Integration Management involves the necessary procedures and tasks to recognize, describe, merge, unify, and organize the different processes and activities related to project management across the various groups involved in the project management process.

The key processes in Project Integration Management are mentioned below.

1. **Create the project charter** — One of the initial steps in project management is to create a project charter. This involves preparing an official document that approves a project or its phase and outlines the initial requirements that meet the needs and expectations of stakeholders.
2. **Develop a project management strategy**— documenting the necessary steps to define, prepare, combine, and synchronize all subordinate plans.

3. **Direct and Manage Project Work**— carry out the tasks stated in the project management plan to achieve the project's objectives.
4. **Monitor and Control Project Work**— supervise, assess, and adjust the progress to satisfy the performance objectives established in the project management plan.
5. **Implement Integrated Change Control**— evaluating all change requests, approving changes, and handling modifications to the deliverables, organizational process assets, project documents, and the project management plan.
6. **Close Project or Phase**— Finish all the activities involved in each of the Project Management Process Groups in order to formally bring the project or phase to an end.

Starting a project and integrating it

Starting a new project is like starting a new business without any planning. It genuinely involves a lot of research, planning, and project execution. The project board's guiding principles have proven helpful in getting a project off the ground. Still, they have also helped project management teams understand how crucial it is to find the ideal partner who will be crucial to the project's success. Every project needs a financial strategy, and the task can only be started exactly as planned with the help of these partners with similar interests. To avoid worrying about finding people while doing errands, you should start by assembling a strong team that can handle the many aspects of the project from the beginning. Even though some project components might need to be generated later, it seems reasonable for each project manager to have the right employees ready to begin working on the components even before their services are needed, they do not need to be paid, but you still need to get the group ready.

The startup also needs to set up a particular origination budget, timeframe, and scope of work that are itemized. Once a profile is created, the different work assignments can be started immediately. The manager must then consider creating and managing each task meticulously. Booking and precise arrangements ought to make this achievable. Ensure nothing is covered and the task is manageable as you finish the planning and booking. When you invest time at the beginning of the project and throughout the mixing, it helps to ensure that the project will proceed without a hitch. The creation of a financial plan is essential, as is the estimation of various initial expenditures. Applying creativity, communication, and workable solutions is also necessary to smooth out the project's usefulness.

At this point, the task starts to be carried out, and the flowchart and various graphs are put in place. There will be numerous positions you need to deal with while organizing a work arrangement, but everything begins with the very first one. Therefore, creating a strong draft is crucial.

Anything that starts is energetic, which is why the beginning of a project is also the most exciting period for the entire team because creativity levels are at an all-time high. This is a fantastic opportunity to get the most out of your team and make sure they contribute as many hours as they can toward the project and develop a more solid working connection. When the project is well-established, the manager can set clear expectations for the task group and anticipate what they should say. The task manager is responsible for creating a work environment that motivates the team members and ensures that they devote all of their available time to the task at hand to produce innovative and excellent results.

Managing Integration

Integration is one of the main parts of the task of the board. This incorporates assembling all the different exercises that should be set up for the smooth working and conveyance of the task. It incorporates getting the elements and sorting out the person, the assertion, the degree, and the arranging expected for the venture to be fruitful. It would be best if you also considered keeping a fallback that will assist you with rolling out the vital improvements if things don’t go as planned.

Project Management Integration

Project the executives joining is only the expected cycle for effective coordination of an undertaking, and different goals must be characterized to finish the task according to the partner's assumptions. These are the three significant cycles concerning the project executive's integration:

- The project plan development
- The project plan execution

Controlling change

Each of these cycles typically communicates with one another and with the cycles that are engaged with the execution of the venture. Each cycle referenced above will require mediation from an individual or perhaps a gathering of people. This section will fill you in regarding the instruments, cycles, and strategies utilized to combine every one of the cycles of venture management.

The advancement of the undertaking plan relies upon the other interaction yields in the arranging stage. This will be useful in making a reliable report that will direct the undertaking control and the execution of the venture. While the underlying draft won't have explicit spans and assets, the last arrangement will have dates set up for each cycle and assets that will be dispensed to every one of the cycles. This venture plan will generally be utilized to do the following:

Help project execution enhance communication between the project manager and the stakeholder. Make sure that you look at the main elements of the project concerning the extent and timing and provide guidelines that will help with project control and measurement of progress

Development of the project plan

The task plan will be created in light of various variables. This plan

will likewise be founded on verifiable information and records of past tasks. The item administrator from those tasks can likewise be counseled in fostering a venture plan for a comparative undertaking. This information is very vital in assisting with the activities and examining choices in the event of hindrances.

Organizational approaches will likewise be viewed while executing the task plan. This implies that the venture plan should incorporate the accompanying attributes:

Managing the quality of the project via process audits and improvement targets noting down a guideline for personnel administration noting down all aspects of the project concerning financial control, including the expenditure expected, the accounting codes, and the disbursement policies

When making a task plan, limitations additionally should be thought about. These limitations should be dealt with, and a fallback must be set up to move past the requirements without an over-the-top hiccup. The undertaking plan will likewise comprise suppositions that will be the key to indicating the beginning and end dates for the task. Every one of the suspicions will, for the most part, have some hazard. It ought not to be excessively far misguided, and this is the place where the ability of the task supervisor comes into the picture.

Methodology of Project Planning

Philosophy is generally an organized methodology that will assist the group with fostering an arrangement that will be straightforward yet far-reaching. The approach will likewise include different gatherings between the partners and the task supervisor. This will assist them with thinking of a thorough arrangement to execute the undertaking successfully.

The ability and information of all partners should also be considered while fostering the last arrangement. The task administrator requirements to invite input from the partners so the colleagues can utilize their experience to their advantage.

The undertaking chief will likewise need to set up a data framework to assist the whole group with imparting flawlessly and straightforwardly. This could be as a CRM or an inside instrument that will work with correspondence and assist the undertaking chief with planning among partners and group members.

Project Plan

The venture plan must be a supported report that will characterize every one of the boundaries used to deal with the execution of the task. This venture plan will be appropriate to everybody engaged with the task, and this will assist everybody with finding out what the courses of events are and the date of finishing. If any progressions are made to the undertaking plan, all partners and colleagues should be quick to be educated regarding it. An undertaking plan ought to incorporate every one of the accompanying components and, at times, a couple more because of the task requirements:

description of the approach by the team to complete the project on time

charter of the project

statement of scope that will include the objectives of the project and the deliverables

work structure that will define the level of control that will be exercised, approximate dates for the start and end of the project, and the responsibilities allocated to each team member. An approximation of the project cost and budgetary constraints. A description of how performance will be evaluated and a timetable for audits. Significant checkpoints in the project's progress, along with deadlines for each.

The key staff that is required for the project

Any risk of constraints that the project manager may predict

The backup plan for each of the risks that are predicted for any open issues or discussions that are pending with the stakeholders

The venture plan can likewise incorporate any supporting subtleties or info from different cycles inside the association. It can also include detailed information regarding the project, such as technicalities and any additional third-party resources needed.

Project Integration Questions

1. You have been hired by a company to be the new Director of Customer Delivery. Ten projects are at various stages of completion, but one project in particular concerns you. You would like to see a document that outlines the information required from a business perspective to assess whether the expected outcomes of this project justifiably warrant the required investment in it. Which of the following documents should you study to understand this for that project?

A. The Project Management Plan.

B. The Project Scope Statement.

C. The Business Case.

D. The Scope Management Plan.

2. Bernie manages projects for a firm that deals with information technology. A stakeholder requests that a significant adjustment be made to one of the projects he oversees, which would result in additional costs and a faster delivery schedule. Bernie had to incorporate the change into his project after the necessary procedure resulted in approving the change request. What ought he to do next?

A. He must ensure that he tracks this change against the project's baseline to know how much it eventually costs.

B. To reflect this change, he must amend the Project Charter.

C. He needs to incorporate the change into the project baseline to track the project properly.

D. He must use the Project Management Information System to ensure the work is performed.

3. You learn of a serious issue while managing a telecommunications project that poses a serious risk to its completion and will almost certainly affect the stakeholders' ability to conduct business. It will take a day to evaluate the issue, and its full effects have not yet been determined. What would be the wisest course of action in this situation?

A. Update the findings in the lessons learned and add them to the organization's OPA.

B. Set up an emergency meeting with the stakeholders and inform them of the situation and that you will need one more day to provide complete information about the problem.

C. Initiate a change request and submit this to the Change Control Board at the earliest.

D. Go through the project charter to check who is authorized to make decisions.

4. A project stakeholder recently raised a change request with you. What does this mean if anything?

A. A. You can go ahead and make the desired adjustment as the project is now in the Direct and Manage Project Work process.

B. Though the project charter is complete, you cannot commence work because you must change the scope baseline.

C. C. Before being put into effect, the change must go through the approval process.

D. Since the change is a defect, it must be repaired right away.

5. Which of the claims, as mentioned earlier, regarding the project management plan is untrue?

A. It is not the document that sanctions authority to the project manager.

B. It does not contain the Communications Management Plan.

C. It contains the performance baseline.

D. It contains a schedule baseline.

6. Because he no longer sees any economic value in the project you are overseeing, the project sponsor decides to end it. What should you do next, exactly?

A. Reassign people who have been working on your project to new projects.

B. Refuse to stop the project since it was already approved and continue the work.

C. Check with your PMO team on how to use the rest of the budget.

D. Initiate closure procedures to close the project and update the lessons learned.

One of your senior developers leaves on indefinite leave while you're heading a software project because of a personal emergency. What should you in this situation do first?

A. Determine how the developer's absence will affect the project.

B. Inform all stakeholders that the project will now be delayed indefinitely.

C. Inform team members that they must work overtime to compensate for the resource loss.

D. Contact Human Resources to hire a replacement.

8. As the project manager for a logistics project, Jeremy is aware of various approved adjustments that are still to be implemented. He must choose how to allocate project resources to carry out these changes. What ought he to do?

A. He should reject the changes because they would delay the project.

B. He should prioritize these changes and then announce them to the team.

C. He should consult the prioritization management plan for guidance on prioritizing new changes.

D. To decide whether to move through with the reforms, he should consult with all parties involved.

9. Which of the statements above regarding the project charter is false?

A. The project charter grants authority to the project manager to manage the project.

B. The project sponsor issues it.

C. It provides a milestone schedule for the project.

D. The project manager must be consulted when it is being created.

10. A stakeholder has just submitted a change request to project manager Jacob. Jacob has a gut feeling that making this adjustment could jeopardize his project's schedule. He convenes a project team meeting and informs them of the urgent need to start change control. Which of the following is not a result of the next process?

A. Change Requests.

B. Project document updates.

C. Project Management Plan updates.

D. Change Request status updates.

11. You oversee a project that is on track and will be finished two days early. But now, a significant stakeholder has contacted you and asked for a significant change in the project that might take a full day to complete.

A. Ask the stakeholder to send an email outlining the change and then make the change.

B. Implement the change since you are already ahead of schedule.

C. Refuse to change until the stakeholder documents it in a Change Request.

D. Let the stakeholders know you are open to the change and ask them to contact the project sponsor also.

12. Dan must choose one of three brand-new ventures. The Net Present Value (NPV) of Project A is $45,000, and it can be finished in a year. The NPV of Project B is $56,000, and it can be finished in 18 months. The NPV of Project C is $100,000, and it can be finished in two years. Which of these initiatives ought he to choose?

A. Project A.

B. Project B.

C. Project C.

D. None. NPV is not a criterion used for project selection.

13. What statement about a work authorization system is false?

A. It authorizes the start of work packages or activities.

B. It is a part of Project Management Information Systems (PMIS).

C. It is not part of an organization's Enterprise Environment Factors (EEF).

D. The WBS dictionary may be used as a part of this system.

14. A client has advised the project manager that the project charter has to be modified. Who is ultimately responsible for determining if suggested changes to a Project charter are necessary? Select the best choice.

A. The project manager.

B. The customer.

C. The functional manager

D. The project sponsor.

15. What exactly does it mean when someone refers to the project manager as an integrator?

A. It implies that the project manager has to integrate different project parts into a program.

B. It implies that the project manager has to integrate team members into one unit.

C. It implies that the project manager has to integrate individual pieces of the project into a coherent whole.

D. It implies that the project manager's role is more limited in a project than that of his team members.

16. One of the very first tasks on a project is creating a project charter, but what can it be used for as it nears completion?

A. To check whether any new change requests should be approved.

B. To establish the relationship between the performing and requesting organizations.

C. To authorize the project manager.

D. To function as a substitute for a contract.

17. Realistic expectations and goals should be used while creating a project management plan. What method of creating a project management plan would be MOST appropriate?

A. After consulting with the project manager, the project sponsor should create the Project Management Plan.

B. After consulting with the senior management team, the project manager should create the project plan.

C. The functional manager should create the project plan after consulting with the manager.

D. D. The project manager should consult the project team for advice before creating the project plan.

18. As a project manager, you've recently learned that a client has requested a change. You know this modification won't influence the project's budget or timeline. What ought you to do now?

A. Put the adjustment into effect because it won't affect the budget or timeline.

B. Determine if there are any potential impacts of the proposed change on other project constraints.

C. Submit the change to the CCB.

D. Reject the change since you have already completed the planning stage.

19. After all technical work has been completed, a project has just entered the Close Project or Phase procedure Which of the following doesn't constitute a part of this process?

A. Closing project accounts.

B. Finalizing open claims.

C. Validate Scope.

D. Completing Lessons Learnt.

20. You've just developed a brand-new project management plan. But before you baseline it, a stakeholder notices an important omission and asks you to adjust the Project Management Plan to consider this. What ought you to do?

A. Ask the stakeholder to submit a change request.

B. Consult with the Change Control Board.

C. Rejecting the request from the stakeholder after informing him what he requested is a scope creep.

D. Make the requested change in the Project Management Plan.

21. When reading about knowledge management for the PMP test, one of your colleagues could not discern between tacit and explicit knowledge. As a result, you instruct her that:

A. Tacit knowledge is the type of knowledge that is difficult to express and comes from experience, whereas explicit knowledge is fact-based knowledge that can be easily codified.

B. Explicit knowledge is the type of knowledge that comes from experience and includes emotions. Still, it is hard to codify, whereas tacit knowledge is fact-based knowledge that can be easily codified.

C. Tacit knowledge is conveyed through pictures and diagrams, while explicit knowledge is conveyed through written text.

D. Tacit knowledge is the knowledge that is internal to an organization, whereas explicit knowledge is that which is obtained from external sources.

22. The Configuration Management System and the Change Control System are essential to project management. What sets the two apart from one another?

A. Both are part of Environment Enterprise Factors.

B. The Change Control System is included in the PMIS, but the Configuration Management System is not. Conversely, the Configuration Management System is a component of the PMIS, whereas the Change Control System is not.

C. The Change Control System mainly deals with the changes to the project baseline, while the Configuration Management System mainly deals with changes in product specifications.

23. Which of the following claims about a change request that has been granted is FALSE?

A. The Direct and Manage Project Work method produced it.

B. The project team plans and carries it out.

B. The cost baseline might alter as a result.

D. The baseline schedule may change as a result

24. You are engaged in one of the numerous initiatives to swap out an existing customer's business support systems with one of your brand's flagship goods. One of your stakeholders submits a change request for your ongoing project when it is in the execution stage. However, after analyzing the requested adjustment, you conclude that it is inconsistent with the goals or specifications stated in your project charter. What would be the best move to make in this circumstance?

A. Revise the project schedule of your project.

B. Evaluate the scope of work for this change with your team's help.

C. Use the information from the requested change to develop a new project charter.

D. Submit the change to the CCB.

25. Out of four projects, a project manager must select the most lucrative one. He discovers that Project A's internal rate of return (IRR) is 20%, Project B's IRR is 25%, Project C's IRR is 36%, and Project D's IRR is 28%. Which project ought he to pick?

A. Project A.

B. Project B.

C. Project C.

D. Project D.

Project Integration Detailed Answers Keys

1. Answer C. The Business Case document provides the necessary information from a business point of view to evaluate whether the expected outcomes of the project justify the required investment.

2. Answer C. After a change has been authorized, the project baseline needs to be updated as soon as possible. This will make the project's tracking with the new baseline accurate.

3. Answer B. The best line of action in this situation is to make the stakeholders aware of the issue. Given that the problem hasn't been fully assessed, a change request isn't the sensible action in this case. The project charter should not be consulted; updating lessons learned is not the appropriate course of action.

4. Answer C. Change requests are only accepted as input into the Perform Integrated Change Control procedure, and after a change has been received, the next step is to get it authorized. The other options are all wrong.

5. Answer B. The Project Management Plan includes every individual management plan, including the Communications Management Plan.

6. Answer D. A project may be abandoned in the middle. But after a project has been canceled, the following step is to follow protocol and start the project's official closure.

7. Answer A. The project manager must decide how to proceed if a resource is unavailable. The first stage is to determine the impact of the absence, quantify it, and then decide how to move forward.

8. Answer B. The project manager must choose the order of importance for the adjustments. The changes cannot be denied since they have already been accepted (i.e., through the Change Control Board). Additionally, there is no such thing as a prioritization management plan, and calling in all the stakeholders would be pointless, given that these changes were already accepted.

9. Answer D. Although not required, the Project Manager may be consulted when developing a project charter. When the project charter is being created, the project manager may be unaware of it.

10. Answer A. Even though there is a lot of irrelevant information in this question, the question only asks which choice does not result from the "Perform Integrated Change Control" process. Change Requests are an input rather than an output in the procedure, as mentioned earlier.

11. Answer C. Each change request must be documented for any new change to go through the Perform Integrated Change Control procedure. Before it is fully documented and submitted to the Perform Integrated Change Process, a new change cannot be implemented.

12. Answer C. Dan should choose Project C because it has the highest NPV. Therefore, the information provided on the number of years for completion is meaningless because NPV already takes timing into account when calculating the value. The last option is untrue because NPV is a reliable economic formula that may be used to choose projects.

13. Answer C. The enterprise environment factors of an organization are thought to include the work authorization system. The other claims are all accurate.

14. Answer D. The project sponsor is in charge of issuing the project charter and ultimately deciding whether any amendments are required.

15. Answer C. When a project manager is referred to as an integrator in project management, it signifies that they combine multiple project activities into a unified whole.

16. Answer A. If a new change request is made after the project has already begun, one way to decide whether it should be authorized is to see if the project charter covers the change. If not, it must be discarded, moved to a different project, or launched on its own. Choices B and C are incorrect since the project charter defines the relationship mentioned and authorizes the project manager at the start of the project (and not as the project is approaching completion). Additionally, a contract cannot be replaced by a project charter.

17. Answer D. This query implies who creates the project management plan, and this is made by the project manager using suggestions from the project team. While the senior management team's suggestions may be helpful, the project's actual team's suggestions are considerably more important for developing a realistic plan because they are the ones who can accurately estimate the quantity of work that needs to be done and the time needed.

18. Answer B. No information is provided regarding the proposed change's effects on the other project constraints, even though it will not affect the schedule or budget. Therefore, before presenting this modification to the Change Control Board, assessing potential effects on scope, quality, risk, and resources (CCB) would be necessary. Requests for changes may be made any time after planning, which is not a cause to deny them.

19. Answer C. Validate scope is not done during the closing process but during the Monitoring and Controlling step. The actions taken at the moment of closure are mentioned in all other alternatives.

20. Answer D. This omission can be included in the project management plan without approaching the CCB, requesting the stakeholder to submit a change request, or treating this as scope creep because the project management plan has not yet been baselined.

21. Answer A. While implicit information, which includes opinions, ideas, and experience, is private and challenging to articulate, explicit knowledge can easily be codified using words, drawings, and numbers.

22. Answer D. Options B and C are erroneous since both the Change Control System and the Configuration Management System are part of an organization's PMIS; however, option A does not demonstrate a distinction. Simply put, the two systems vary in that the Configuration Management System handles changes to product specifications, whereas the Change Control System handles changes to the project baseline.

23. Answer A. Change requests that have been approved are inputs rather than outputs into the Direct and Manage Work Process.

24. Answer C. The suggested change cannot be incorporated into the current project since it is outside the scope of the project charter. Therefore, starting this as a separate project would be the best course of action, and a new project charter needs to be written for this. All of the alternative solutions try to address the issue as a component of or an addition to the current project.

25. Answer C. The best alternative is Project C, which has a 36 percent internal rate of return. The internal rate of return determines how profitable a project is.

CHAPTER 5:
Project Scope

Educational Section Regarding the Topic Project Scope

Project Scope Management is the process of identifying and controlling all the work required to complete the project successfully while ensuring that only the necessary work is included. The main challenges associated with project scope management are described in the following sections:

- The client provides a high-level vision for the project, but stakeholders are unable to articulate specific objectives and deliverables, or they provide conflicting viewpoints.
- Conflicting requirements due to different interpretations of the same statement by various individuals.
- A commitment is made to the client without fully understanding the application portfolio.
- Project teams may consider additional work to be a change request despite the client's insistence that it is part of the original scope.
- The project is suddenly running out of time, and additional requirements are emerging while development work is ongoing.

Project Scope Management includes the following procedures to ensure that the project is completed successfully with all necessary work and no unnecessary work. This is the definition as per PMBOK.

The term "scope" refers to two different aspects of the project:

• Product scope: This refers to the attributes and capabilities of the project's outcome.

• Project scope: This refers to the work required to produce the project's outcome, including all desired features and functionalities.

The project plan is used to evaluate project scope, while demand is used to evaluate product scope.

Product Lifecycle: - A product lifecycle is undertaken to launch a product. A product lifecycle may have several projects and operations.

Project Scope Management

Following are the key processes in Project Scope Management

1. **Plan Scope Management** – developing a scope management strategy, which outlines how the project's scope will be determined, verified, and managed
2. **Collect Requirements**—The process of defining and documenting stakeholders' needs to meet the project objectives
3. **Define Scope**— creating a thorough description of the project and product
4. **Create WBS**— The method of breaking down project work and deliverables into smaller, more manageable components.
5. **Validate Scope**— the procedure for formally accepting finished project deliverables
6. **Control Scope**— the procedure for keeping track of project and product scope developments and controlling scope baseline alterations.

Management Of the Project Scope

The major steps in project scope management are as follows: 1. Plan Scope

1. Management - The process of producing a scope management plan that outlines how the project scope will be determined, verified, and controlled
2. Gather Requirements—Identifying and capturing stakeholders' requirements to achieve project goals.
3. Identify the project's scope and create a thorough description of the final product.
4. Develop an Effort Breakdown Structure (WBS) to break down project deliverables and work into smaller, more manageable components.
5. Validate Scope—The procedure for formally accepting the project deliverables that have been completed.

6. Control scope—The procedure for keeping track of the project and product scope's progress and controlling modifications to the baseline scope
7. The sections of this chapter that follow provide a detailed explanation of these procedures.

Management Of the Plan Scope

To produce a scope management plan, which outlines how the project scope will be determined, verified, and controlled, is known as the scope management process.

The main benefit of this procedure is that it provides directions and guidance on managing the project scope throughout the project's lifecycle.

Now, let's examine the inputs, tools, techniques, and outputs involved in this process.

Plan Scope Management: Inputs

The scope management plan, which outlines how the project scope will be determined, verified, and controlled, is developed with the aid of subsidiary plans included in the project management plan that affect the project scope's planning and management.

Project Charter: It lists the high-level project requirements that the scope

a management plan can refer to.

Enterprise environmental elements: - The organizational culture, infrastructure,

personnel administration, market conditions, and other enterprise's environmental

factors might have an impact on the plan scope management process.

Organizational process assets include policies, procedures, historical data, lessons

gained, knowledge base, and other items that can have an impact on the planned scope

management process.

Tools and Techniques - Plan Scope Management Expert Judgment - Input from knowledgeable and experienced parties is included here. Expertise in creating scope management plans may be provided by individuals or groups with specific education, knowledge, skills, experience, or training.

Meetings: To create the scope management plan, project teams may attend meetings. These sessions may be attended by the project manager, project sponsor, selected project team members, chosen stakeholders, individuals responsible for any of the scope management processes, and any other relevant parties.

Take Requirements In

The identification and documentation of the demands of the important stakeholders is the process's main goal. Both functional and nonfunctional requirements represent the demands.

Cartoons about projects, like the one below, are well-liked and frequently criticize the poor work done in the field of requirements collection.

The following are the benefits of a thorough requirement collection process:

- Greater acceptance of the project's deliverables by key stakeholders; • Avoiding
- scope ambiguities later in the project's lifespan.
- Developing a solid solution that satisfies the users' needs.
- The product of this process, the requirements document, serves as the basis for constructing the work breakdown structure, the timetable, the cost estimation, and procurement-related decisions.
- The process of locating and documenting the needs of project stakeholders is known as requirements gathering. It is described in this way in the PMBOK. During this phase, you will learn about a variety of tools and techniques that support the requirement collection procedure.

Let's review the process' inputs, tools, techniques, and outputs.

Collect requirements as inputs.

Plan for Scope Management The scope management plan clarifies the process through which project teams will choose the categories of needs that must be gathered for the project.

Management of Requirements The techniques that will be utilized to identify and record the stakeholder needs during the requirements collection process are provided in the requirements management strategy.

Plan for Managing Stakeholders To evaluate and adjust to the level of stakeholder participation in requirements activities, it is necessary to understand the stakeholder communication requirements and the level of stakeholder engagement.

Project charter: The objectives of the project are outlined in the project charter, which is a document. This serves as the requirements document's guiding document.

The list of all stakeholders is called the stakeholder registry. All of the stakeholders' requirements must be gathered utilizing a variety of methods, including surveys, questionnaires, and interviews.

Resources & Methods: gathering requirements.

Interviews: The stakeholders are being spoken with one-on-one to pinpoint their precise demands. Focus groups:

This requires discussing needs with a group of people.

Facilitated workshops: This method is structured, and a moderator guides the group while they brainstorm. The cross-functional teams collaborate and choose shared objectives and goals.

Joint Application is used, for instance, in the software development industry.

Development (JAD) sessions. The Quality Function Deployment (QFD) method is used in the manufacturing sector to identify the crucial features of a new product.

Creative group techniques:

The following are a few group creative techniques:

- Delphi Technique: In the Delphi Technique, answers to specific queries are requested from anonymous users. A moderator shares everyone's thoughts, and after further iterations, a list of demands from all parties is reached.
- Mind maps: This method helps you see how the thoughts are related.
- Affinity Diagrams: These are useful tools for organizing similar ideas into groups.
- Brainstorming: This method of gathering requirements involves a group sitting together and developing new ideas.
- The Nominal Group Technique is a method of brainstorming where participants write down their ideas and then vote on the top ones.
- Decision-making uses many criteria. a method for evaluating and ranking numerous ideas that make use of a decision matrix to Describe a methodical analytical approach for developing criteria such as risk magnitudes, uncertainty, and valuation.

Specify Scope

The creation of a thorough project scope statement is crucial to the project's success because it establishes the baseline understanding of the project's key deliverables among all of its stakeholders. It also outlines the project's goals, requirements, limitations, and assumptions, as well as the risks associated with the project's scope and the acceptance standards for the finished output.

"Defining scope" is the process of thoroughly describing the project and its outcome. The PMBOK describes it thus.

Let's review the process' inputs, tools, techniques, and outputs.

Project Scope Questions

1. You have been responsible for managing the creation of a brand-new product that is the most recent innovation in the industry; after further improvements, it was recognized as a distinct class; other design elements classify the product as state-of-the-art at an affordable price. This demonstrates how product attributes are developed over time. Yet careful coordination with the is required. You choose to determine the extent to which the project scope will change while reviewing scope change requests on a project you manage. Which project document will you need to compare to?
2. You were recently appointed project manager for a sizable utility project, and you have a steering committee meeting scheduled to discuss the project's goals, development, and deliverables. You should thus prepare one of the documents listed below.
3. You are in charge of organizing a team to create project selection and priority criteria for your organization, which has a lot of projects on the go. What elements of a project selection model are most important? Ensuring that previously developed items are effectively maintained is one of your company's goals. As a result, you put in place a proactive maintenance system for each product in use. A system like that should?
4. You are in charge of a project with three teams spread across three sites. The company knows that team members sometimes respond better to their functional supervisors than to you as the project manager. The first step should be?
5. The best management model would be Management by Objectives because of it.
6. You recently completed the concept phase of a ground-breaking medical initiative for which you are the project manager. The product for this stage is the?
7. Instead of creating a WBS, one of your subcontractors created a bill of materials for a project component. Your suggestion, however, constituted a change in the project's scope. Does this serve as an illustration of a modification request that results?
8. You created the scope description, WBS, and project plan for your project as the project manager. However, you decided to set up a project scope change control system because you realize that scope change is unavoidable. That's it?
9. The work package is a?

10. Your team is creating one of two parts for the utility system that you are managing. For a potential subcontractor, you must create a description of the second portion and the necessary documentation.
11. You are in charge of a project whose scope statement was approved by the project sponsor. They did request a change to the project's scope, though. This explains a change in the scope that, at the very least?
12. Your current project is abruptly canceled, and you are given a new one. However, notwithstanding the possibility that this might occur occasionally, shouldn't a project manager be appointed?
13. You were compelled to alter the scope of your project due to new government regulations. The project's aims and goals thus needed to be modified in various ways. The planning materials for the project have been updated as necessary. What should you do next, exactly?
14. The predicted value of every new product must outweigh its development costs, according to a directive from your management. Your idea is in the concept stage; this is an illustration of?
15. To outline the necessary work and gauge the scope of your new project, you choose to start with a WBS. Your business, however, does not have any WBS templates. Creating the WBS should be your first action. You were just put on a different project team. The team is engaged in a new project for the business that requires long-term resource commitment. The project charter, which must be published by the projects?
16. You are in charge of a group creating a new line of goods. However, the new product concepts from your team don't align with the organization's skill sets. You must return and remodel the product by the management's guidelines.
17. Your employer has tasked you with working on a project abroad. A law in the nation where the project is based mandates you to hire people from a particular ethnic background. What limitations does this represent?

Project Scope Detailed Answers Keys

1. Careful coordination of the progressive elaboration of product attributes with appropriate scope definition and declaration is required. **Project Planning**
2. The WBS defines the scope baseline, providing the basis for any change in the project. **Project Planning**
3. The scope statement is the stakeholder's mutual understanding of the project's scope. **Project Planning**
4. The selection criteria should reflect the company's strategy and objectives**. Project Initiating**
5. Projects have a beginning and an end by default; maintenance is an ongoing effort, and the project's lifecycle begins with initiation and ends with closure. Maintenance Is not part of the lifecycle. **Project Initiating**
6. The project charter provides a framework for the project; it may help resolve conflicts but may not eliminate them. **Project Initiating**
7. Management by objectives focuses on the goals and objectives. **Project Initiating**
8. The project charter provides official recognition of the project's existence and authorizes the project manager to assign resources. **Project Initiating**
9. Whereas, the WBS is a collection of project elements used to define the project's scope, the bill of materials pertains to physical components. **Project Controlling**
10. The project's overall change control plan must be integrated with scope change control. **Project Controlling**
11. In a project or WBS, a work package is the smallest or lowest level of work division. **Project Planning**
12. The buyer, in this case, the project manager, provides the statement of work. **Project Initiating**
13. A scope change is always expected but should be part of scope change control management. **Project Controlling**
14. The project manager should be chosen during the project's initiation phase. **Project Initiating**
15. Notifying stakeholders should be done if a major change in project objectives occurs. **Project Controlling**
16. The project team's options will be restricted by constraints. **Project Initiating**
17. The WBS is breaking down the project into small deliverables. **Project Planning**
18. An executive from outside the project should issue the project charter at a level that is appropriate for the project's requirements. **Project Initiating**

19. Assumptions are factors that are true, real, or certain. **Project Initiating**

20. The terms and conditions are legal requirements in any contract that must be respected. **Project Initiating**

CHAPTER 6:
Project Quality

Educational Section Regarding the Topic Project Quality

In this chapter, we will discuss the topic of Project Quality Management, its definition, and its key deliverables.

Some of the key examinable terms in this chapter include:

- Statement of Work
- Quality Policy Framework
- Quality Milestones and Deliverables
- Schedule Baseline Requirements and Total Potential Project Support (TPPS)
- Change Control Processes
- Change Request Management, Change Request Tracking System, Change Request Portfolio Management Tools, etc.

Project Excellence

The primary factor that a task leader needs to focus on is the nature of the venture conveyed and the task being completed on schedule if they want to have a good reputation in the industry. The task manager must ensure the project is carried out accurately and by the many details provided. Job quality defines the assumptions and details, but it also helps the team learn how to overcome new challenges and concentrate on delivering high-quality work that promotes repeat business.

It is the responsibility of the project manager to develop an execution plan that not only ensures that the employees and the collaboration are well on the task dependably but also that they are roused throughout. Process inconsistencies are something that could cause the project to go south. The project manager should keep this type of detail in mind while planning the project's timetable and budget to maintain high quality. Convenient leaves and breaks are also occasionally essential. The underlying partner and those who might be crucial to the project and might consider donating or buying must esteem this project abstract.

Project Team Having the correct people or group working on the project is crucial, regardless of how big or little the assignment is. To properly manage and complete the job, the group must possess the necessary talent. There should always be a few members on a task team who are essential to the group.

Recruiting and communication

You must hire the right people if you want any project to be completed successfully. A strong human resources department that can hire employees from within the company, independent contractors, and even third-party employers is the best approach to finding these people.

Since it enables people to associate, communication is essential. It will be impossible for the venture to succeed without a good specialized technique. Having a group available to handle this correspondence is highly advised, regardless of whether it involves face-to-face meetings or even regular virtual chats.

Enterprise Environmental Factors

Think of enterprise environmental factors as if you are asking yourself: "What will influence my project?" Many things can influence your project, such as:

Attempting to memorize the PMBOK® Guide cover-to-cover is not a good use of your preparation time. Instead, think carefully about the concepts you must study and focus on the larger picture. One of these ideas is the enterprise environment.

In the real-working world of project management, terms like "enterprise environmental factors" are not used (or rarely used, at best). However, as a project manager, you are expected to use the concept, and PMI expects you to understand the term and the influence of enterprise environmental factors on project management.

Let's put enterprise environmental factors into perspective. For example, if you get to work Monday and get assigned a new project, one of the questions you want to answer is, "What things are going to influence and impact this project?" You want to start thinking about these things before you start planning. Below is an overview of some of the enterprise environmental factors, with examples, to help you better understand their influence:

Organization's culture, structure, and governance

PMI is big on highlighting the importance of cultural awareness. You need to know how different cultures and styles affect your project. For example, an organization's culture is likely to impact the project scope and requirements, affecting how a project will run. The framework for decision-making and oversight are key aspects of organizational governance and structure that contribute to project success.

Government or industry standards

There are many factors to consider regarding government or industry standards, and much depends on the type of industry in which your project is involved. For example, the financial services industry sees constant change and evolution of standards, impacting how reporting processes and policies must be implemented. Continuing with that same example, new laws and regulations resulting from a new government standard can significantly impact a financial services project. Examples include reporting standards to the government or even accounting practices.

Infrastructure

With infrastructure, consider things that help you define the physical structures that affect the organization's operational capabilities. Examples of infrastructure questions may focus on areas such as; what is your office space capacity? What equipment and sources are available to you? What are the current communication features, furthermore?

Existing Human Resources

Don't confuse this enterprise environmental factor with the human resources management knowledge area or activities in the planning and executing process groups. Note the examples above for existing human resources, such as determining if certain skills and core competencies can be leveraged.

Marketplace conditions

The part of a project that market conditions may impact depends on the project type. For example, economic conditions may need to be factored into your budget if you are managing a construction project. Also, you may need to consider the cost of steel or the fluctuations in currency. If you have a global project that involves several different currencies, this could potentially affect the project scope, cost, etc.

Risk tolerances

The risk tolerance of your stakeholders matters and impacts the decisions you make early in the project. You need to know whether your project sponsor is risk-averse because it impacts how you manage certain project parts. Your stakeholder's risk tolerance level impacts everything from scope definition, requirements planning, schedule, budget, etc.

For instance, if you and your spouse renovate your house to include a media room. Isn't it crucial to understand that your partner is risk-averse? This is crucial, without a doubt! This may mean your spouse has reservations about the skylight you want to be cut into the roof. As a key stakeholder, your spouse's concerns about the potential of the skylight leaking when it rains are an important consideration that should be factored into your project scope planning.

Politics (Political Environment)

For many projects, the impact of internal and external politics will be a big factor. Consider the situation where you are in charge of an oil and gas project. In that instance, you might need to take into account the political sway of regional, national, or even foreign administrations.

PMIS (Project Management Information System)

The PMIS is not just your project software application. The PMIS refers to everything managing your project – from your repository, disposition, storage, project servers, etc. The PMIS effectively includes all the tools and templates you will use to manage your project from beginning to end.

Key Takeaway: Enterprise Environmental Factors

Enterprise environmental factors show up in most process inputs in the PMBOK. When studying, think about examples or real-life situations to help you recall ways a specific enterprise environmental factor may apply to the process with which you are being tested. Use the examples in this book, or think of your examples. As noted earlier, examples help you put exam concepts into perspective and put you in a better position to answer questions that may appear on your exam.

Project Quality Questions

1. In addition to implementing quality standards like ISO 9000, your organization also has its own set of requirements for quality. Every project your company works on contains a quality policy in line with the company's standards. On all projects, it offers both internal and external quality assurance.
2. You recognize that mistakes happen in your project while planning and implementing quality assurance systems.
3. You are creating a superior, durable product as part of your project. You carried out quality assurance and control throughout the project and created a project quality management plan. You know that some rework would be required, but the management of your company does not support it. What would you say about reworking?
4. You are in charge of a project to create a utility product, and you predict that 20 resources will be required. Senior resources are more productive than younger resources, although both types are scarce. What method should be employed to choose the best combination of resources?
5. As a member of an expert team tasked with creating a system to decrease patient wait times in hospitals, you were tasked with identifying issues and suggesting and putting up solutions. What would be the best strategy in this scenario to aid in identifying the elements contributing to this problem?
6. What distinguishes variable sampling from attribute sampling?
7. You oversaw a project that brought a new process into a manufacturing company; this new process had a few mishaps occur in several locations at roughly the same time. Which of the following strategies would your project team employ if you had decided to look into the issue and ask the team for help analyzing the new procedure?
8. What does a controlled process often mean?
9. Can the following, with one exception, be used to explain quality management?
10. It is easier to carry out quality control procedures with a basic understanding of statistical process control. Which of the following must the team fully comprehend?
11. Because long-term contracting exists, project quality control is crucial to this arrangement.
12. The methods to employ for keeping track of the number of mistakes or flaws that have been found and the number that have remained undetected are?

13. You chose to utilize flowcharting as a project manager for a new product because you wanted to comprehend some design elements to foresee quality difficulties.
14. You must create a project management plan, which includes a quality management plan, after being allocated to a new project. What would your first action be while creating this plan?
15. The normal anticipated deviation of a process is? Process control limits are stated in expected deviations from the mean.
16. As a project manager, you know how crucial quality control is to your project. However, you also understand that excellence comes at a price, and your project has a limited budget. One strategy to lower the price of quality is to?
17. It should be directed as a way to establish and maintain a culture of continual development, right?
18. Typically, products are checked as they leave the line or at key points. Rework and repair are both pricey choices for damaged products. To reduce the cost of rework, you choose to incorporate inspections at different phases of product development. May inspections also be requested?
19. Your management has ordered a quality audit after each project phase. Is this an audit component of the company?
20. What is involved in quality control?

Project Quality Detailed Answers Keys

1. Quality control improves the efficacy and efficiency of the project and offers additional advantages to its stakeholders. The project's planned and organized operations assure us that it will meet all applicable quality standards. **Project Executing**
2. The conventional wisdom holds that people make mistakes. **Project Controlling**
3. In some application areas, additional effort can be required. The project team must make every effort to reduce rework, though. **Project Controlling**
4. This method is employed to determine which factors impact the final result most. **Project Planning**
5. Ishikawa diagrams or fishbone diagrams, often cause-and-effect diagrams, show how different factors interact to produce potential issues or outcomes. **Project Controlling**
6. Determined by attribute sampling is compliance. The level of conformance is measured via variable sampling. **Project Controlling**
7. Control charts assess if a process is stable or experiencing performance problems. **Project Controlling**
8. Only after approved change procedures are processes able to be altered or modified. **Project Controlling**
9. All management and staff levels are concerned with quality. **Project Planning**
10. The fundamental elements of statistical process control are sampling and probability. **Project Controlling**
11. Long-term connections with customers encourage vendors to invest more in process and quality improvement since they have a better chance of recouping their expenditures. **Project Planning**
12. Using mathematical methods, trend analysis predicts future outcomes based on past performance. **Project Controlling**
13. Using flowcharts, the project team may identify and create solutions for potential quality issues. **Project Controlling**
14. The top management's formally announced general aims and quality direction are included in the quality policy. **Project Planning**
15. when a sample's measured findings are within 3 standard deviations. It is reasonable to infer that more than 99 percent of the items fall within that range because the sample normally represents the total population. **Project Executing**

16. Statistical sampling can greatly lower the cost of quality control by selecting the desired portion of a population for inspection. **Project Controlling**
17. The initiative to foster creativity, pride, cooperation, and the pursuit of knowledge is driven by executive management. **Project Executing**
18. Inspections involve procedures used to check whether outcomes meet specifications. Reviews and walk-thoughts are other terms for inspections. **Project Controlling**
19. A project's quality assurance function creates methods to help assess if quality criteria are being fulfilled. **Project Executing**
20. Monitoring project activities and outcomes involves evaluating performance and ensuring completeness. **Project Controlling**

CHAPTER 7:
Project Resources

Educational Section Regarding the Topic Project Resources

Project Resources are the resources (both human and non-human) that will be used to implement a project. In this chapter, we will discuss the topic of Project Resource Management, its definition, and its key deliverables.

Some of the key examinable terms in this chapter include:

- Resource Management Plan
- Project resource breakdown structure
- Resource breakdown structure

Managing Human Resources

A tremendous job of undertaking chiefs includes ensuring they get the right individuals to deal with the errand. This includes remaining in consistent contact with the human asset office and circling back to occasionally the recruiting and advancement methodology. It additionally includes dealing with the whole team.

Managing Communication

Various individuals will be engaged with the task, and it will contact the existence of numerous individuals en route right from the day the venture starts until its culmination. For any task to be finished in a smoothed-out way, it is important to have solid relational abilities to produce data concerning appropriation, execution, and revealing and the administration of various segments of the venture proficiently. Taking everything into account, one likewise needs to ensure that they are in steady contact with the outside partners as well as individuals who are essential for the team.

Project Resources Questions

1. You have been given the responsibility of leading a project that will have a significant impact on numerous crucial business efforts. You understand that maintaining total control over the project's resources is necessary for success. What kind of project organization do you need to set up for this project?
2. Which of the following guidelines for team building should you follow?
3. In a projected organization, you oversee a project and answer to a vice president who supports it. Which of the following best summarizes the project manager's relative influence in this situation?
4. Which of the following things contributes the most to team building and communication?
5. When many projects are carried out inside the functional organization, significant obstacles develop because?
6. Effective team building can lead to various outcomes, but the main outcome is?
7. Some signs of troubled projects may go overlooked when an endeavor has problems. Except for one, have you observed any of the following signs of poor performance in your project team?
8. There are different types of management; what is it termed when there is little to no communication between the project manager and the project team for a freshly formed team?
9. A project's success depends on the team's development, and you know this as the project manager. As a result, you should assess the technical environment in which your team works. Can you find these details in the?
10. What is the main factor in a matrix organizational setting that triggers conflict?
11. The project manager's interest may aid the team's development in the group. What would be a wise suggestion for a project manager to demonstrate personal interest in?
12. You saw several unfavorable team dynamics, such as tardiness, absenteeism, and poor performance. To involve the team in various sporting and entertaining activities, you decided to organize an event. You're planning this event primarily to get better.
13. One of the primary limitations that could impact how the project team is organized is?
14. You are a member of a team working on a project where the project manager, although an authority in his field, often solicits input from others. What do you

think we should do? This is the most likely response he will provide to a question. Which of the following best describes his leadership style?

15. In an organizational system, a project manager and coordinator play independent functions.
16. What would be a constraint on the hiring process?
17. What type of management approach best describes a project manager who frequently makes decisions without considering team members' input?
18. Management promised to give you all the resources you need to finish the project on schedule because it is so important to the company's future. It would help if you prioritized it as you started this undertaking.
19. Strong matrix, balanced matrix, and weak matrix are the three types of matrix organizations. In an organization, the matrix structure refers to the?
20. What is the main tenet of team development?

Project Resources Detailed Answers Keys

1. All project team members report directly and completely to the project manager under a projectized organizational structure. Compared to any other project organizational structure, they have total control over these resources and have more authority over them. **Project Planning**
2. Initiating the team-building process early in the project is essential to establish the right tone and prevent the formation of negative habits and patterns. **Project Executing**
3. In an organizational structure that is projectized, the project manager possesses complete authority over the project. **Project Planning**
4. Colocation involves consolidating the team in one place to improve their capacity to work together. **Project Executing**
5. Conflict results when a small number of resources must be split between several initiatives. **Project Planning**
6. Improved performance is aided by team development. **Project Executing**
7. Excessive ineffective meetings are a significant contributor to failure. **Project Executing**
8. While this approach may work well for strong, self-directed teams, it can be isolating and frustrating for teams that require guidance. **Project Planning**

9. The technical environment in which the team works is described in the project plan. **Project Executing**
10. When multiple parties share related responsibilities, unclear boundaries can arise due to ambiguous role definitions and work boundaries. **Project Executing**
11. Celebrating milestone events like birthdays and anniversaries can show team members that you care about them and promote a sense of belonging. **Project Executing**
12. Team building results in better team performance, eventually leading to better project performance. **Project Executing**
13. The project team's options are limited by constraints and external circumstances over which the team has no influence. **Project Planning**
14. Shared leadership is practiced by allowing the project team to assume as much of the leadership position as they are willing to. **Project Executing**
15. Compared to the project coordinator, the project manager is relatively higher in the organizational hierarchy. **Project Executing**
16. Staffing assignments may be governed by policies, processes, or guidelines established by the project's participating organizations. **Project Planning**
17. Autocratic managers are only interested in their information. **Project Executing**
18. The success of a project depends on an efficient team, so both the project manager and the team must start team-building exercises immediately. **Project Executing**
19. In a matrix organization, the phrase alludes to the project manager's dominance over the project team. **Project Planning**
20. The foundation of team development is individual development. **Project Executing**

Chapter 8:
Project Risk

Educational Section Regarding the Topic Project Risk

This chapter will discuss the topic of Risk Management and its Risks.

Some of the key examinable terms in this chapter include:

- Risk Management
- Probability and Impact Analysis
- Risk Assessment and Response Planning
- Risk Management Process
- Risk Communication and Reporting

Project Risk Detailed Answers Keys

1. When creating a risk management plan, it is important to establish the organization's risk threshold. While the customer or sponsor may have different thresholds, the project team should use the performing organization's threshold as the standard to evaluate the effectiveness of risk response plan implementation. **Project Planning**
2. Risk generally remains high during the initiating and planning phases. The highest risk usually occurs during planning and implementation. However, the risk is lower during project implementation and closeout as remaining unknowns are becoming knowns. **Project Planning**
3. Uniqueness means that the past is not always a perfect guide to the future. **Project Planning**
4. While the knowledge of the project team may be valuable, it's worth noting that recollections are less dependable compared to other forms of documentation. **Project Planning**
5. Brainstorming is a commonly used method for identifying risks. **Project Planning**

6. Risk responses that have not been pre-defined prior to the actual occurrence of the risk event are referred to as workarounds. **Project Controlling**
7. Monte Carlo analysis is a statistical tool that supports various types of analysis. **Project Planning.**
8. Choosing to face the consequences of a risk event is known as risk acceptance and not avoidance. **Project Planning**
9. The probability of both events is calculated by multiplying the probability of both (the first event) by the probability of (the second event). **Project Planning**
10. WBS identifies all the work that must be delivered; it is the right tool to identify potential sources of risks. **Project Planning**.
11. Some risks are unknown-unknowns, meaning there is no way of knowing when and if they occur. **Project Controlling**
12. Sensitivity analysis helps determine which individual risk has the most potential impact on the project plan. **Project Planning**
13. EMV = ($2M × 50%) + (–$1M × 20%) = ($1M) + (–$200,000) = $800,000. **Project Planning**
14. An external entity performs risk audits to control risks. Risk reviews can be done anytime by the project team. **Project Controlling**
15. Acceptance means accepting the consequences of a risk. **Project Planning**
16. The probability of the risk by its impact is the risk score that can also provide a way to compare risks. **Project Planning**
17. A contingency or a fallback plan is a corrective action to bring performance back if the selected plan does not work. **Project Controlling**
18. A decision-tree analysis is used to support the best selection from alternatives. **Project Planning**
19. A Checklist is a tool for risk identification. A checklist can be developed based on historical information or the team's knowledge from similar projects. Reviewing the checklist should be a formal step of every project closing procedure. **Project Controlling**
20. Risk mitigation involves actions by the project team to reduce the probability of occurrence or impact of a threat. **Project Planning**

Management of Risk

Risk management in project management involves various procedures such as risk management planning, risk analysis, risk identification, and risk control.

The following are the main tasks involved in the risk management process.

1. Organize risk management.

It is the process of outlining how risk management tasks should be carried out for a project.

2. Recognize risk

It is figuring out which risk could impact the project most. The documentation of current threats is part of this procedure.

Risk management strategy, project scope statement, cost management plan, schedule management plan, human resource management plan, and scope baseline will all be used to assess risk.

Stakeholder register, activity cost estimates, activity length estimates, project documentation, and procurement documents

Organizational process assets, the enterprise environmental factor, and the communication management plan

Both qualitative and quantitative risk assessments should be carried out.

- Prepare risk mitigation strategies
- Keep an eye on and manage hazards

A risk registry will be the procedure's outcome.

3. Conduct a qualitative risk analysis

Before further investigation or action is taken, risks are ranked according to their likelihood of occurring and potential consequences. It aids managers in reducing uncertainty and focusing on risks with the highest priority.

Early project planning should include risk management since it can affect many factors, including cost, time, scope, quality, and procurement.

The following are some of the inputs for qualitative risk analysis: risk management plan and baseline scope.

Enterprise environmental variables, organizational process assets, and the risk register

Project document updates would be the result of this stage.

4. Quantitative risk assessment

The process of using mathematical calculations to evaluate the potential impact of identified risks on project goals is known as quantitative risk analysis. This analysis aids in making informed decisions that reduce project uncertainty.

The inputs for this stage include the risk management strategy, cost management plan, schedule management plan, risk register, enterprise environmental factors, and organizational process assets.

Updates to the project documents will be the outcome.

5. Prepare risk reactions

A plan to address risks is essential to minimize threats and maximize opportunities towards achieving project goals. The risk response plan takes into account the criticality of risks based on factors such as schedule, budget, project activities, and management approach.

The inputs to planning risk responses include the risk management strategy and risk register.

Although the results are

- Updates to the project management plan
- Updates to project documents

6. Manage Risks

The process of controlling risks includes activities such as keeping track of previously identified risks, identifying new risks, assessing risks, and monitoring residual risks.

Project management strategy is one of the inputs for this stage.

Work performance information, work performance statistics, and work performance reports

This step would result in the following:

- Work performance data
- Change requests.
- Updates to the project management plan

Updates to project papers and organizational process assets

Management of project procurement

The methods of acquiring goods required to run a firm are included in project procurement management. The company may be a service provider, buyer, or seller.

In project procurement management, the control of external contracts and the employment of non-project team members are also included.

Plan Procurement Management consists of four stages: Plan Procurement Management, Conduct Procurements, Control Procurements, and Close Procurements.

The following are the inputs for the plan procurement management:

- Teaming agreements, risk register, and scope baseline
- Project schedule, activity cost estimates, and cost performance baselines.
- Risk-related contract decisions
- Environmental aspects of the business
- Resources for organization processes

Execute the procurement procedure

The procurement process includes choosing a supplier, getting seller answers, and awarding contracts.
The advantage of performing procurement processes is that they align the expectations of internal and external stakeholders through documented agreements.
Project management strategy, procurement documents, and source selection criteria are among the inputs used in the procurement process.

- Project documentation
- Seller proposals
- Qualified seller list
- Purchase decisions
- Agreements for teams
- Resources for organization processes

Control purchases

It is the process of keeping track of a contract's performance and adjusting per the rules. It will ensure buyers and sellers comply with the legal agreement's procurement requirements.

Project management strategy, procurement paperwork, agreements, and approved modification requests are among the inputs for control procurements.

Reports on employee performance; data on employee performance

The output consists of project management plan updates, work performance information, and change requests.

- Updates to project documents
- Updates to organizational process assets

Closed purchases

Documenting agreements and other papers for later use is the goal of this phase.

The tool's input includes the project management plan and the procurement documents.

This tool's output consists of • Closed procurements

- Updates to organizational process assets

Control stakeholder involvement

Stakeholders play a crucial role in the outcome of any project due to the influence of their decisions. To begin the stakeholder management process, it is important to pinpoint the individuals, organizations, or groups that could affect the project and analyze their expectations. Regular communication with stakeholders is also essential to fully understand their needs and desires.

Finding the Stakeholders

The current task involves identifying the entities, whether they are groups, individuals, or organizations, that hold the potential to impact the final results of the project. This technique can be employed by the project manager to identify the appropriate stakeholders.

Stakeholder Management in a Plan

It involves developing a plan to incorporate stakeholders at various project life cycle stages. It outlines a concise, practical plan for communicating with project stakeholders.

A project management plan, stakeholder registration, and enterprise environmental considerations are among the inputs for Plan Stakeholder Management.

- Resources for organization processes

The results of this include a plan to manage stakeholders.

- Updates to project documents

Control stakeholder involvement

Engaging with stakeholders is essential to understand their expectations, resolve issues, and promote their active involvement in the project's operations. This approach empowers the project manager to successfully execute the project without infringing on the stakeholders' decision-making authority.

During this phase, the stakeholder management plan, communication management plan, change log, and organizational process assets are utilized as inputs. The resulting output of this stage includes an updated project management plan, issue logs, change requests, and project documents.

- Revisions to assets related to organizational procedures.

Engaging Stakeholders in Control

The process includes monitoring stakeholder engagement in the project and making necessary adjustments to enhance their involvement as the project progresses. Inputs for this stage consist of a project management plan, issue log, work performance data, and project documents, while the outputs include information related to work performance and change requests.

- Updates to the project management plan

Updates to project papers and organizational process assets

Summary

In summary, risk management involves various procedures such as risk planning, analysis, identification, and control. To manage risk effectively, an organization can follow steps like risk identification, qualification, response, monitoring, and control.

Procurement management includes the processes of acquiring goods necessary for an organization's operations and monitoring contract performance in accordance with regulations.

Effective communication is crucial to ensure stakeholder involvement in a project, as their decisions can have a significant impact on the project delivery.

Project Risk Questions

1. The main goal is to determine how well the team members' execution performed based on the?
2. Which stages of the project lifecycle are the riskiest?
3. Because of this, projects are particularly prone to risk.
4. Historical information is the least trustworthy type of information that can be utilized to identify risks.
5. You've just been tasked with organizing a project's risk identification efforts and creating a list of probable dangers. You are aware that many strategies might be employed. However, which one is more usually employed in risk assessment?
6. Is a solution?
7. Most statistical simulations of budgets, schedules, and resource allocations employ which of the following analyses?
8. Except for one, the following statements concerning risk mitigation are true.
9. Danger event 1 has a 70% likelihood, and risk event 2 has an 80% probability. How likely is it that both occurrences will occur if they are independent?
10. Why is the WBS used in the risk identification procedure in the first place?
11. Why is management reserve used?
12. What is the most basic type of risk analysis?
13. What is the anticipated financial value of a new company with a 50% probability of making $2 million in profit and a 20% chance of losing $1 million?
14. What distinguishes a risk audit from a risk review?
15. You are in charge of a project where a huge number of appliances for one of the biggest merchants in the world are housed in a data center. You have developed a backup plan to run your business from a different city in a crisis due to the danger of storms. This is what is known as a risk response.
16. How does the Risk Score function?
17. What is an illustration of corrective action in risk management?
18. What is employed in the decision-tree analysis?
19. Applying the knowledge gained from earlier initiatives to boost project management effectiveness is crucial. Therefore, it is crucial to review the during project closure operations.

CHAPTER 9:
Agile Project

Educational Section Regarding the Topic Agile Project

This chapter will discuss the topic of Agile Projects and their related Agile Methods.

Some of the key examinable terms in this chapter include:

- Agile Project
- Agile Methodology
- Agile Software Development
- Development sprints and iterations
- Collaboration
- Scrum framework

Overview of Methodologies

The many different demands of developing work call for a different approach to handling the project management elements. As you read through this book, you'll learn about the basic elements and principles of the Agile Method and how you can use these principles to guide your team through your project.

The common challenge among Agile Project Leaders is that the different methodologies may apply to a project differently. Sometimes, a methodology doesn't come into play during a project. Then there are other times when you may use various methodologies in varying capacities for a single project. You will surely learn more about the principles which govern Agile Software Development. However, you'll need to use your leadership and communication skills to determine which methodology fits your project and which fits your team.

Agile Methodologies include, but are not limited to:

- Scrum – A lightweight framework that emphasizes small increments of work, driven by productivity and simplicity.
- Lean – Utilizes value stream mapping to deliver high value to the customer or end-user and is highly adaptable.
- Extreme Programming or XP – Focused on speed and continuous delivery, commonly utilized for software improvement.
- Crystal – Regarded as the most flexible Agile Method, it prioritizes communication and team reflection to identify what worked and what didn't.
- DSDM – A method that concentrates ondelivering the "useful 80% part of the system in 20% of the time."
- Feature Driven Development – Uses a feature-based model list to drive the iterations and development process.
- Kanban – A visual approach to work management, typically employed in conjunction with other methodologies. Project progress and future tasks are monitored through work tracking.

Again, when developing an Agile Project, you are not limited to a single methodology. Using grab portions from different Agile Methodologies and use them together. Alternatively, you may use a single methodology. How and what you use is determined by you and the Agile team. As the project manager, you're likely the champion for the company and the project meaning that you are the bridge between the Agile Team and the desired result. With proper project management and Agile Techniques, you can help your team develop highly functional software through proven techniques and systems.

Scrum

The Scrum methodology is widely used in various organizations, employing an iterative approach to identify key features and objectives before each sprint. Its main aim is to minimize risks and enhance value. One of the tools used in Scrum is a storytelling technique to specify feature performance and testing. The Scrum team then delivers small portions through sprints while addressing any questions that may arise early on.

Compared to the Waterfall Model, Scrum is distinct due to its collaborative and iterative approach. Unlike Waterfall, Scrum doesn't require extensive documentation, making it easier to modify unsuitable features. Regular sprint retrospectives ensure proper communication and understanding between developers and testers. A Scrum Master supervises the project progress.

Fast iterations in Scrum make it ideal for teams working on a project with customers and stakeholders that expect an early working product release. Participation from stakeholders and product owners helps the team make necessary changes.

Overall, Agile development is crucial for organizations and companies to embrace. However, new players might get overwhelmed with the vast content on Agile available on the internet.

Agile is a highly effective methodology for building software and products, providing a flexible approach that empowers individuals. To ensure success with Agile approaches, the following important features should be present:

- Shared understanding of processes and objectives
- Commitment
- Collaboration between all stakeholders
- Transparency
- Readiness to exchange information

Agile Software Development Techniques

Nonstop Integration

This process entails team members collaborating on a product and merging their individual developments with the rest of the team. Each integration is assessed to identify any issues with the integration process, and corrective measures are implemented to resolve the problem.

Test Driven Development

In this coding process, a brief development cycle is repeated several times. The developer designs an automated test case to assess a new function, creates concise code to pass a specified test, and subsequently revises the new code to comply with new standards.

Pair Programming

One programmer acts as the driver and the other as the programmer, and they work together at a single workstation, scrutinizing each line of code inputted.

Design Patterns

In software engineering design, it is vital to incorporate reusable solutions. Design patterns offer solutions to specific issues that can be utilized in multiple scenarios. These patterns are a formal practice that can be executed by programmers within an application. Object-oriented patterns illustrate object and class relationships and interactions, without defining the object classes and applications used.

Domain-driven design

This approach involves coordinating intricate designs with a particular model, prioritizing domain logic in the project, and initiating a collaborative process between domain experts and the technical team to minimize conceptual difficulties. Domain-driven practices offer a set of methods that aid in design decisions and accelerate software projects dealing with complicated domains.

Code refactoring

The process of code refactoring aims to enhance the internal structure of a software system without impacting its external features.

Agile Project Questions

1. An agile methodology is best suited for which environment. Select from the following?

   A. A simple software development project where the requirements are mostly undetermined

   B. A simple software development project where the requirements are firmly set

   C. A complex software development project where the requirements are mostly undetermined

   D. A complex software development project where the requirements are firmly set

2. The product owner can attend, but he is not required to attend which of the following meeting?

   A. Iteration retrospective

   B. Release planning meeting

   C. Daily stand-up meeting

   D. Iteration planning meeting

3. What is the difference between Wideband Delphi and Traditional Delphi?

   A. The experts are surveyed in a Traditional Delphi, whereas experts are interviewed in Wideband Delphi

   B. The experts are surveyed in a Wideband Delphi, whereas experts are interviewed in Traditional Delphi

   C. Wideband Delphi is used to estimate a range, whereas Traditional Delphi is used to survey the experts

   D. Traditional Delphi produces a range of estimates, whereas the Wideband Delphi is used for surveying the experts

4. Which of the following best represents the 3 Scrum pillars?

   A. Collection, Retrospective, Adaptation

   B. Communication, Planning, Adaptation

C. Collection, Sustainability, Adaptation

D. Visibility, Inspection, Adaptation

5. The smallest set of functionalities that has value to the customer is known as?

A. A user story

B. A minimal marketable feature

C. A story point

D. A function

6. An agile team member estimated she could complete a user story in three days if not assigned other tasks. This is an example of a?

A. Communicating at an ideal time

B. Timeboxing the user story

C. Following Agile principles

D. Using Wideband Delphi

7. Which of the following describes "continuous integration?"

A. Releasing software frequently

B. Frequent testing of all features

C. Agile practices are reminded to all team members

D. Checking in new codes daily

8. The team has released a build that does not comply with the organization's coding standards. What does this mean?

A. The agile team is responsible for the delay in the delivery outlined in the product roadmap

B. The agile team will incur technical debt

C. The agile team violates agile principles

D. The agile team is working towards self-organization

9. Who is responsible for keeping the agile team focused?

A. The product owner

B. The PMO

C. The coach

D. The team must discipline themselves

10. Which one of the following describes a sponsor's most important role in an Agile project?

    A. To help define product value

    B. To provide product backlog

    C. To approve a project plan

    D. To provide the project's financial resources

11. The Agile team had completed half of the 4-week iteration when they started getting new change requests from the customers. The new change requests were due to changes in business direction, and this situation created unwarranted anxiety in the Agile team. As an Agile PM, how will you curb the anxiety while continuously providing value to the customer in this situation?

    A. Since Agile is all about changes and adaptability, you will consider those changes and include them in the current iteration

    B. Display all change requests that come in the backlog

    C. Increase the iteration by 2 weeks to incorporate changes

    D. Cancel the current iteration and work on a new iteration incorporating the requested changes

12. In Agile projects, the project backlog is prioritized using many different factors. From the following select three.

    A. Iteration velocity

    B. Business value

    C. Project risks based on features

    D. Business value and risks

13. All of the following represent a product owner's responsibilities. Select three.

    A. Participate in planning

B. Ensuring the team has a common vision for the Agile project

C. Funding the Agile project

D. Making decisions to ensure a better ROI

14. In Agile, a roadmap is created for stakeholder information. How do you describe a product roadmap?

A. A list of features and screens

B. A pictorial view of release candidates based on prioritized features

C. Instructions for the deployment of features in a backlog

D. A backlog prioritization scheme based on team velocity

15. Many ____________ create a release that provides a complete software application.

16. Which one of the following best describes the key characteristic of an Agile contract?

A. It is based on a time and materials agreement

B. It can accommodate changes

C. It is based on incentives and rewards

D. It is based on firm requirements

17. The incomplete or newly-identified _________________ are queued back in the _______________.

18. Ideal and calendar days are time-related terminologies used in Agile methodologies. Which one of the following statements describes ideal days?

A. The ideal day represents a period of productive work without any disturbances

B. Both are the same. The terms are interchangeable

C. Calendar days represent a typical work day that includes normal interruptions

D. Typically calendar days are not equal to ideal days

19. A term used in Agile projects is known as risk-adjusted backlog. From the following, which one best describes why a risk-adjusted backlog is created?

A. To prevent the team from risks

B. To avoid keeping the risk register separate from the feature register

C. To keep the Agile team focused on risks and features

D. To ensure that the features with higher risks are worked on in the early iterations

20. The Agile project team has some conflict, and you are the Agile PM diagnosing what level of conflict the team is experiencing. You notice that statements such as once again, so and so have no clue is becoming a common theme. What level of conflict is the team experiencing?

    A. Level 1

    B. Level 2

    C. Level 3

    D. Level 4

Agile Project Detailed Answers Keys

1. The answer is C. An Agile project is well suited for a complex IT project where the requirements must be decomposed into user stories, and allowances are made for continuous changes.
2. The answer is A. In an iteration retrospective meeting, the Product Owner can attend, but it is not required.
3. Answer is C. Wideband Delphi is used to estimate a range, whereas Traditional Delphi is used to survey the experts.
4. Answer is D. Scrum has three pillars. Visibility, Inspection, Adaptation
5. Answer is B. A Minimal Marketable Feature (MMF) is the smallest deliverable that can add value to the users.
6. Answer is B. Timeboxing is confining the product backlog to be performed within a set period.
7. Answer is D. Continued integration means the developed code must be integrated daily (Checking in new codes daily).
8. Answer is B. Technical debt is when the Agile team chooses to implement code quickly even though it does not yet comply with organizational coding standards.
9. Answer is C. In XP Agile methodology, a coach is responsible to keep the agile team focused.

10. Answer is D. In Agile the project sponsor provides the finances for the project. The sponsor is not the product owner, who provides the product backlog and product value.
11. Answer is B. You add the new changes to the product backlog. They will be reviewed and prioritized by the Product Owner, and then they will be given to the Agile team in the next iterations. Answer "A" is wrong, since the iteration commitment is done by the Agile team. You cannot add to the iteration that is in progress. Answer "C" is wrong because you cannot increase the iteration duration. Answer "D" is wrong since an iteration's cancellation can only be done by the Product Owner.
12. Answers are B, C, and D. The project backlog prioritization factors are: Business value, Project risks based on features, and Business value and Risks.
13. Answers are A, B, and D. A product owner's responsibilities include: Participating in planning, Ensuring the team has a common vision for the Agile project, and Making decisions to ensure a better ROI. Answer C is wrong since the Agile project funding is the responsibility of the Sponsor, not the Product Owner.
14. Answer is B. A product roadmap shows what releases are planned and what relevant features they would have.
15. Answer is: Many **iterations** create a release that provides a complete software application.
16. Answer is B. The Agile manifesto welcomes changes.
17. Answer is: The incomplete or newly-identified **requirements** are queued back in the **backlog**.
18. Answer is A. Ideal days represent the period of productive work without any disturbances.
19. Answer is D. The product backlog is sorted by the risks and associated feature value. The features with higher customer value and higher risks are delivered in earlier releases.
20. Answer is C. The team is making sweeping statements and assumptions, generalizations, and suppositions. This is a level 3 conflict characterized by Leas' Conflict model. Leas' conflict model describes 5 levels of conflict: (1) A problem to solve, (2) Disagreement, (3) Contest, (4) Fight (5) World War

CHAPTER 10:
Mock Exam

Educational Section Regarding the Topic Mock Exam

In this chapter, we will discuss the topic of the Mock Exam.

Some of the key examinable terms in this chapter include:

- What is PMP?
- Project Management Body of Knowledge (PMBOK)
- What are some objectives of PMBOK?
- What are high-level processes as defined in PMBOK?
- What are the components of a project plan?

Describe the PMP exam.

The Project Management Body of Knowledge (PMBOK) ® Guide, on which the PMP test is based, lists tasks in the five project management domains of initiating, planning, carrying out, monitoring, controlling, and closing.

There are 200 multiple-choice questions in the test. Twenty-five of the 200 questions are "sample" questions, which do not affect the test-score takers in any way. The remaining 175 questions comprise the test taker's final score.

What Are Your Strengths in Project Management?

More specifically, in this step, we'll help you decide which project management processes and knowledge areas you should initially concentrate on. The fifth edition of the PMBOK® Guide lists 10 knowledge categories and five process groups.

These are the five process groups:

1. Initiating

2. Planning

3. Executing

4. Controlling and Monitoring

5. Closing

These are the ten Knowledge Areas:

4. Project Management Integration

5. Project Scope Administration

6. Time management for projects

7. Cost Management for Projects

8. Quality Assurance in Projects

9. Human Resource Management for Projects

10. Managing Project Communications

11. Managing Project Risk.

12. Purchasing Project Management

13. Managing Project Stakeholders

Each knowledge area comprises a given number of project management processes, each with clear inputs and outputs created using a particular set of tools and methods. We all start this journey at a different beginning point since we have various project management backgrounds. This straightforward reality suggests that, even though completing the PMP Certification is our common goal, our learning objectives should inevitably differ.

In my professional career, I could always rely on experienced financial controllers and a well-rounded procurement team. Still, when I embarked on this adventure, I knew the cost and procurement management processes would push me. Therefore, I realized I needed to concentrate more on these two topics when preparing for the PMP.

Therefore, we want to accomplish two goals in this second step:

Determine which process groups and areas you should ideally concentrate on, or at the least, spend a little more time on, to a) raise awareness of them; b) begin drafting a high-level timeline for your journey.

What Are Your Learning Objectives?

The rating obtained in the previous exercise should now help you define your learning objectives. Naturally, I was hoping you could focus on the areas in your rating that are less. However, it would help if you didn't overlook the areas in which you excel.

Please, remember the following: to pass the PMP Exam, you must be not only proficient in a couple of process groups, but you must also be proficient in most of them!

Our next step is drafting a template for your learning journey. As I introduced earlier, everything we do in life can be considered a project. Thus, it would help to consider this journey your professional self-improvement project with one clear goal: passing the PMP exam. And as with any other project, we must draft a high-level plan before kicking off any activities and developing the various anticipated deliverables.

The Ten Knowledge Areas

According to the *PMBOK® Guide*, "*a knowledge area represents a complete set of concepts, terms, and activities that make up a professional field, project management field, or area of specialization.*"

Even though you may be an expert in a particular knowledge area, I strongly encourage all candidates for the PMP Exam to spend a minimum of one to three days reading and studying each area. The next 10 sections highlight important concepts and formulas you should master before taking the exam.

Project Integration Management

As you go through this section of the PMBOK® Guide, keep in mind that the Project Integration Management procedures are designed to be integrative.

Their purpose is to identify, define, combine, unify, and coordinate the different procedures and tasks within the Project Management Process Groups.

Project Integration Management involves making trade-offs and decisions based on competitive alternatives and resource availability and manages the interdependencies between knowledge areas.

The Project Integration Management processes are:

The first Integration process defines the high-level scope of work, developing the foundational document of the project: the **Project Charter**. Once approved by the project sponsor, the project is formally authorized. This gives the assigned project manager the authority to acquire resources and initiate the project activities.

Next is to develop a more detailed plan for the project: the **Project Management Plan**. This plan defines how the various project activities are coordinated. This plan integrates all the subsidiary plans that are outputs of the other project management planning processes.

The project plan remains a theoretical concept until it is put into action. Thus, as the project manager, the next step in Project Integration Management is to Direct and Manage Project Work, which involves supervising and executing the work outlined in the plan, as well as implementing any approved modifications. These processes are integrative and necessitate constant monitoring and control of the work. To achieve this, Work Performance data is collected, transformed into Work Performance Information, and communicated to stakeholders through Work Performance Reports. This promotes transparency throughout the project.

In these monitoring and controlling activities, the project manager must pay attention to any changes affecting the project goal and implements a well-defined **change control management** only to integrate approved changes into the project scope of work.

Last, as the project continues, and because a project is a temporary endeavor, the responsibility of the project manager is to ensure that the project sponsor accepts all project deliverables to finalize all activities across all project processes, thus documenting lessons learned, and enriching the organizational process assets, and formally completing and closing the current phase or project.

Mock Exam Questions

1. Kai earns a token for every two correct responses. What schedule of reinforcement is this?

   a. Continuous

   b. Fixed-Ratio

   c. Fixed-Interval

   d. Variable-Interval

2. Danny is working with Jake on identifying animals. Danny teaches this by sitting at a table and showing Jake 3 different pictures. Two of the photographs are not animals, while one is an animal. Danny provides the SD, "Show me the animal." Jake will receive a token on his board if he identifies the correct picture. If he does not respond, then Danny will provide a prompt. Which teaching procedure is Danny using?

   a. Natural Environment Teaching

   b. Discrete Trial Training

   c. Prompt Fading

   d. Chaining procedure

3. Stevie loves animals, so his mom took him to the zoo for the day. Stevie was excited to go to the zoo! While at the zoo, Stevie was smiling and laughing while watching the animals. Throughout the day, Stevie's mom pointed to random animals and asked, "What animal is that?" What teaching procedure is Stevie's mom using?

   a. Discrete trial training

   b. Stimulus control transfer

   c. Prompt fading

   d. Natural Environment Teaching

4. Billy and his RBT are playing with toy cars. The RBT has a red car and a blue car in her hand. When Billy says, "I want a car, please," the RBT asks, "Which color?" What type of teaching procedure is this an example of?

    a. Discrete trial training

    b. Chaining procedure

    c. Incidental Teaching

    d. Mand training

5. This procedure breaks a skill down into smaller, more manageable steps.

    a. Discrete trial training

    b. Task Analysis

    c. Natural Environment Teaching

    d. Shaping

6. ____________ occurs when some behaviors are reinforced while others are not reinforced.

    a. Discrimination Training

    b. Prompting

    c. Discrete Trial Training

    d. Shaping

7. Tom is teaching Archie to identify a dog. Tom provides reinforcement when Archie points to a picture of a dog and says, "dog." Tom does not reinforce when Archie points to a picture of a cat and says, "dog." What is this an example of?

    a. Discrete Trial Training

    b. Discrimination Training

    c. Stimulus control

d. Natural environment teaching

8. Prompt delays, prompting fading, and stimulus fading are all examples of…

   a. Generalization

   b. Maintenance

   c. Stimulus control transfer procedures

   d. Prompt hierarchy

9. Mia would like to increase Charlie's independence by tying his shoes. Typically, she will provide hand-over-hand assistance immediately after giving the vocal SD, "Tie shoes." However, today, she waits 10 seconds before assisting. What method is Mia using?

   a. Prompt fading

   b. Stimulus fading

   c. Prompt delay

   d. Shaping

10. While teaching her client to wash his hands, Sarah initially uses full physical prompts, then decreases her assistance until she finishes washing his hands independently. This is an example of a?

    a. Prompt fading

    b. Stimulus fading

    c. Task analysis

    d. Discrimination Training

11. _______________ is referred to as being able to keep a skill over time

    a. Maintenance

    b. Generalization

c. Stimulus control

d. Discrimination

12. Everly's dad is bald, wears glasses, and has a short beard. Not only does she say "Daddy" when she sees her dad, but she also calls every other bald man who wears glasses and has a short beard "Daddy." What is this an example of?

    a. Overgeneralization

    b. Response generalization

    c. Stimulus control

    d. Discrimination Deficits

13. Anthony has difficulty remembering what he needs to do in the morning before school, so his dad lists everything Anthony needs to complete (e.g., eating breakfast, brushing his teeth, getting dressed, packing a bag, etc.). Dad hangs the list on the wall for Anthony to reference. This list is another example.

    a. Task Analysis

    b. Maintenance

    c. Generalization

    d. Discrete Trial Training

14. Shaping is referred to as ____________________.

    a. Reinforcing successful approximations of the behavior until the desired behavior is reached

    b. Maintaining a skill over time

    c. Emitting a response under various stimuli

    d. Transfer control of behavior under one stimulus to the control of another

15. Discrete Trial Training (DTT) occurs in a ___________ environment and is ___________.

    a. Highly Structured, therapist-led
    b. Loosely Structured, therapist-led
    c. Highly structured, client led
    d. Loosely structured, client led

16. The following are examples of behaviors that can be shaped, EXCEPT…

    a. Riding a bicycle
    b. Walking
    c. Talking
    d. All are considered examples of behavior that can be shaped.

17. Mikey has difficulty attending to DTT instructions at the table during ABA therapy sessions, and he often will get up from the table, move around in his seat, and whine when the tasks are too challenging. Currently, the only reinforcement system in place is random breaks that Mikey can earn at the discretion of the RBT. Which of the following is the best strategy the RBT can implement to increase the likelihood of Mikey attending during sessions?

    a. The RBT can implement a token economy.
    b. The RBT should block any attempts to get up from the table
    c. The RBT should reduce the duration of the break every time Mikey gets up from his seat or moves around in his chair
    d. All of the options

18. Which is not considered a component of the behavior reduction plan?

    a. Target behavior
    b. Replacement behavior

c. Crisis protocol

d. Client diagnosis

19. ____________________ are appropriate skills that are taught to individuals that serve the same function as the problem behavior.

a. Replacement behaviors

b. Maintenance goals

c. Function behaviors

d. Target behaviors

20. Every time Lily cries, her mom hugs her. When mom gives a hug, the crying increases. Now, every time Lily wants a hug from mom, she calls. What may be the function of the crying behavior?

a. Sensory

b. Escape

c. Attention

d. Tangible

21. ____________________ is a function of behavior maintained by access to preferred items, toys, activities, or food.

a. Sensory

b. Escape

c. Attention

d. Tangible

22. ____________________________ are environmental variables that alter the effectiveness of a stimulus serving as a reinforcer.

a. Motivating operations

b. Antecedent manipulations

c. Preferred stimuli

d. Natural factors

23. Ross is having difficulty focusing on tasks at the table, so for every other token he earns, the RBT gives Ross a mini M&M. This strategy effectively increases Ross's focus until after lunch when Ross no longer wants the M&Ms. What should the RBT do?

a. Switch up the reinforcer

b. Only give an M&M for the last token Ross earns

c. Stop giving M&Ms

d. Continue providing M&Ms for every other token

24. The teacher wants to reduce the number of times his students get out of their seats, so he praises them when they sit in their seats. This is an example of…

a. DRO

b. DRA

c. DRI

d. DRH

25. Gestural, physical, vocal, and visual are all types of…

a. Prompts

b. Stimuli

c. Techniques

d. Shaping procedures

26. Jordan will curse at his teacher when he does not want to do his work. The following are strategies the teacher can use to reduce the behavior EXCEPT…

a. Teach Jordan to ask for a break

b. Implement a token system to reinforce when Jordan complies with work

c. Place Jordan in time-out every time he curses

d. Ignore the cursing

27. Every time Ava cries, her dad gives her his iPad. When dad realized that the iPad might reinforce Ava's crying, he decided to change. He now no longer gives her the iPad when she cries and, instead, ignores the behavior. This is an example of...

    a. Extinction

    b. Negative Reinforcement

    c. Negative Punishment

    d. Positive Reinforcement

28. Which of the following is not an example of extinction?

    a. Whenever Jeffrey engages in attention-seeking tantrums, his mom gives him a disapproving look.

    b. Liz places an armed guard on Mattie's arm to prevent injury from self-stimulating scratching behavior.

    c. Dad ignores his son's attention-seeking crying behavior

    d. Every Tuesday, you watch your favorite reality tv show. However, the cable went out today, and now you can't watch your show.

29. Your 17-year-old client, Devon, does not engage in aggressive behaviors during the session but has engaged in aggression toward his parents. There have been concerns about Devon's mental health; he was previously hospitalized. However, this was over three years ago, and he has since remained stable. During today's session, Devon's mood was flat, and he seemed disengaged. His appearance is disheveled, his hair is unkempt, and he has a pungent body odor. He confides in you that he has homicidal thoughts toward his parents and plans to act on those thoughts the next day. Based on

this information, you feel Devon is an immediate threat to others and himself. What is the best way to respond to this scenario?

a. Call 911 or local authorities immediately.

b. Contact your BCBA immediately.

c. Evaluate the client to determine if homicidal ideation is valid, and make a decision on how to proceed with getting your client immediate help

d. Document the incident in your note, and then inform the BCBA during supervision

30. Julian engages in severe self-injury in the form of punching his head. He wears a helmet to block self-injury up to 700 times daily. However, Julian learned to remove his helmet to engage in self-injury. A crisis protocol was established with instructions on responding to the behaviors. The RBT is certified in Professional Crisis Management (PCM) and utilizes physical intervention strategies when behaviors escalate. Today, Julian removed his helmet and hit his head so hard that he lost consciousness and had a seizure for 1 minute. What should the RBT do?

a. Call 911

b. Perform CPR

c. Suggest that mom bring Julian to the hospital

d. Wait until Julian regains consciousness, then continue the session.

Mock Exam Answers Keys

1. **Correct Answer: Fixed-Ratio** Fixed-Ratio schedules are those in which reinforcement is provided after a set number of responses.
2. **Correct Answer: Discrete Trial Training** (DTT) teaches skills in a therapist-led structured environment. In DTT, there is the instruction or SD (antecedent), a response (behavior), and reinforcement (consequence). DTT's goal is to transfer the skills to the natural environment eventually.
3. **Correct Answer: Natural Environment Teaching** (NET) sessions are child-led. Teaching opportunities are based on the motivation of the client. In this scenario, Stevie is motivated to go to the zoo because he loves animals. Mom uses Stevie's motivation to teach Stevie the different types of animals in the natural environment.
4. **Correct Answer: Incidental Teaching** Incidental teaching occurs in the natural environment to facilitate communication, but the client must initiate the learning opportunity. The environment may or may not be contrived to elicit the initiation, but the skill is taught only if the client initiates the response. In this example, Billy asks for a car, and the RBT uses that as an opportunity to facilitate communication by having Billy discriminate which color car he'd like to play with.
5. **Correct Answer: Task Analysis** A task analysis breaks a skill down into smaller and more manageable steps. It can be used for multistep skills like tying shoes or brushing teeth. These skills can be broken down even further based on your client's needs!
6. **Correct Answer: Discrimination Training** occurs when teaching the client the difference between 2 or more stimuli. When implementing discrimination training, you reinforce one behavior but not the other. For example, if your client is learning to discriminate between colors, you would reinforce when they correctly label "red," but not when they incorrectly label "red."
7. **Correct Answer: Discrimination Training** This is an example of discrimination training. Discrimination training occurs when teaching the client the difference between 2 or more stimuli. In discrimination training, you reinforce only the correct response. In this case, Tom reinforces only when Archie correctly labels the dog. When Archie incorrectly labels the dog, Tom does not reinforce it
8. **Correct Answer: Stimulus control transfer procedures** are examples of stimulus control transfer procedures. The transfer of stimulus control occurs when a behavior originally evoked by one SD comes under the control of another SD. Prompt fading involves fading prompts so that the behavior eventually occurs without prompts

and only under the control of the SD. Prompt delays occur to allow time for the behavior to happen without the need for prompting. Stimulus fading is used to fade aspects of the stimulus.

9. **Correct Answer: Prompt fading** Mia uses a prompt delay when she waits 10 seconds after providing the SD to prompt Charlie. Delays are a type of prompt fading procedure.
10. **Correct Answer: Prompt fading.** Prompt fading is when one systemically fades the prompts given to an individual to promote independence.
11. **Correct Answer: Maintenance** occurs when one maintains a skill over time.
12. **Correct Answer:** Overgeneralization occurs when the behavior under stimulus control is too widespread. For example, one may associate a stimulus with another based on similar characteristics. In this scenario, Everly thinks all bald men wearing glasses and short beards are her dad.
13. **Correct Answer: Task Analysis** - A task analysis breaks a skill down into smaller, more manageable steps. It can be used for multistep skills like tying shoes or brushing teeth, and it can also be used to help complete a routine. In Anthony's case, many steps are needed to complete his morning routine. The list that dad creates is a task analysis, as it breaks down each task Anthony needs to complete before going to school.
14. **Correct Answer: Reinforcing successful approximations of the behavior until the desired behavior is reached** - Shaping refers to the reinforcement of approximations of behavior until the desired behavior is reached.
15. **Correct Answer: Highly Structured, therapist-led** - DTT occurs in a highly structured environment. Targets are contrived and therapist-led.
16. **Correct Answer: All are considered examples of behavior that can be shaped.** - All are examples of behaviors that can be shaped. With bike riding, you can shape the behavior by first riding a tricycle, then adding training wheels to a bike, then riding the bike without training wheels. For walking, you reinforce rolling over, crawling, standing up, and walking. With talking, you reinforce approximations, then single words, shorter sentences, and more complex sentences.
17. **Correct Answer: The RBT can implement a token economy.** - The key word in this scenario is increase. To increase a behavior, you need to look at a reinforcement system. In this scenario, token economies can be effective reinforcement systems because the reinforcement is immediate. Yes, the RBT could block the client from getting up from the table (e.g., response blocking), but response blocking decreases a behavior, not increases it. Taking away time from the client's break (e.g., response

cost) is a punishment procedure to reduce the behavior. Please note that the BCBA is the one who decides what reinforcement vs. punishment procedures to use. Punishment is always used as a last resort.

18. **Correct Answer: Client diagnosis -** You typically will not see the client's diagnosis in a behavior reduction plan.
19. **Correct Answer: Replacement behaviors** - Replacement behaviors "replace" the function of the behavior with more appropriate behavior. For example, if an individual screams every time they want attention, a replacement behavior may request attention appropriately by tapping another's shoulder or saying, "excuse me."
20. **Correct Answer: Attention** - Hugs are a form of attention. The hugs reinforce Lily's crying behavior.
21. **Correct Answer: Tangible -** Tangible is a function of behavior. This is when behaviors are maintained by access to something physical, like toys, food, activities, or other tangible items.
22. **Correct Answer: Motivating operations** - Motivating operations (MOs) alter stimuli's effectiveness as a reinforcer. MOs can be broken down into establishing operations (EO) vs. abolishing operations (AO). An EO (e.g., thirst) increases the value of the reinforcer (e.g., water), while an AO (e.g., satiation) decreases the value of a reinforcer (e.g., food).
23. **Correct Answer: Switch up the reinforcer** - The RBT should switch up the reinforcer. The motivating operation (MO) has changed the effectiveness of the M&Ms as a reinforcer. Ross may be too satiated to want any more food, so the RBT should try to find a different reinforcer that may be more motivating to Ross.
24. **Correct Answer: DRI** - DRI (differential reinforcer of incompatible behavior) reinforces behavior that cannot occur simultaneously as the target behavior. In this scenario, sitting cannot co-occur as standing or out-of-seat behavior. The teacher uses a DRI procedure when he reinforces his students to sit in their seats instead of being out of them.
25. **Correct Answer: Prompts** - All of these are examples of prompts. Other prompts include modeling, partial physical, and positional.
26. **Correct Answer: Place Jordan in time-out every time he curses** - Although time-outs are punishment procedures intended to reduce behaviors, the punishment does not match the function. Jordan wanted to get out of work, so the teacher putting him in time out gave Jordan what he wanted (e.g., a break from work). This may only reinforce the behavior of cursing.

27. **Correct Answer: Extinction** - This is an example of an extinction procedure. Extinction is when reinforcement is withheld from a previously reinforced behavior.
28. **Correct Answer: Whenever Jeffrey engages in attention-seeking tantrums, his mom gives him a disapproving look.** - Extinction procedures are when reinforcement is withheld for previously reinforced behavior. In this case, Jeffrey's mom giving him a disapproving look when he cries may only reinforce the behavior, as the behavior is maintained by attention.
29. **Correct Answer: Call 911 or local authorities immediately.** - Call 911 or the appropriate local authorities right away! RBTs and BCBAs are not mental health providers, and we are not qualified to rule out suicidal or homicidal ideations. In this case, you must call the appropriate authorities, especially if this client has a history of hospitalizations and mental health.
30. **Correct Answer: Call 911** - This is an emergency, and you need to call 911. After you call 911, contact your BCBA.

CONCLUSION

I've said it before, and I'll say it once more. The PMP is not an impossible test to pass; however, it calls for self-control, commitment, patience, and focused effort.

It would be best if you took full-length mock tests to help you prepare for the exam, in addition to the practice questions in this book and the end-of-chapter questions you would have practiced while studying for the PMP exam. You will need to become used to working on questions for extended periods to prepare yourself for the exam. Sitting for 4 hours at a stretch while tackling 200 problems is mentally and physically taxing.

Through this book, I've done my best to provide you with a set of well-planned and meticulously produced practice questions that will offer you some exposure to the types of questions you might anticipate on the PMP. However, this should not be seen as a promise or assurance of your success, and your efforts ought to go far beyond what is included in this book. Any result, whether favorable or unfavorable, ultimately depends on your talent, unwavering dedication, and overall effort in preparing for the exam.

Made in the USA
Columbia, SC
23 November 2024

47425554R00065